Creative Novel Writing

CREATIVE
NOVEL WRITING

ROSELLE ANGWIN

ROBERT HALE · LONDON

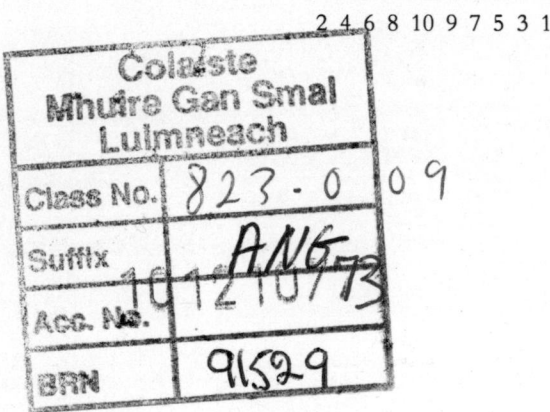

Typeset in North Wales by
Derek Doyle & Associates, Mold, Flintshire.
Printed in Great Britain by
St Edmundsbury Press Limited, Bury St Edmunds
and bound by
WBC Book Manufacturers Limited, Bridgend.

This book is offered with love and thanks to all those who made it through to the end of the Novel course in Plymouth through the winter of 1997/8, without whom it would not have been possible.

Acknowledgements

Acknowledgement is made for passages quoted in the text:

Extracts by permission of Fourth Estate Ltd from *The Shipping News* by E. Annie Proulx © 1993 by E. Annie Proulx.

Extracts of approximately 345 words from pp.90–1 and 127 from *As I Walked Out One Midsummer Morning* by Laurie Lee (Penguin Books, 1971) copyright © Laurie Lee, 1969. Reproduced by permission of Penguin Books Ltd.

The author and publisher would also like to acknowledge other books quoted in the text: *The Way to Write*, by John Moat and John Fairfax (Elm Tree Books 1981), lines from the Introduction by Ted Hughes; *Inner Work* by Robert Johnson (Harper & Row 1989); *The Horse Whisperer*, by Nicholas Evans (Bantam Press 1995, Corgi 1996); *Separation*, by Dan Franck (Editions du Seuil, Paris, 1991, Black Swan 1995); *The English Patient* by Michael Ondaatje (Bloomsbury 1992, Picador 1993); *Aspects of the Novel*, by E.M. Forster (Edward Arnold 1927, Penguin 1990).

Gratitude is due to the inspiration that has also come from lectures at Dartington by Lindsay Clarke and Ben Okri, and their books.

The author would particularly like to thank the participants who brought such enthusiasm, generosity and commitment to her course 'A Novel in Two Terms', out of which grew this book; and also Jeannie Arbuckle, Lyn Browne and Chris Tooke for their permission to use extracts from workshop exercises.

Contents

Introduction

Storytelling goes back, as far as we can tell, to the beginnings of human life on this planet. Storytellers are keepers of wisdom; they weave spells which feed the human soul. In Old Welsh, the same word is used for both storytelling and instruction or guidance. The storyteller was a seer.

The novelist, of course, is carrying on this tradition, albeit through the written rather than the spoken word. If you have chosen to write a novel, it is presumably because you feel you have a story worth telling. The purpose of this book is to enable you to find the most imaginative and effective way to express it.

Perhaps it's important, as writers, to ask both why we write, and why we read. The most obvious answer to the latter, of course, is to do with entertainment, amusement, even escapism – to pass the time. But reading also has a deeper purpose, to do with increasing our knowledge of the world and of ourselves. We read to learn, to inform ourselves, to expand our understanding and awareness, to reassure ourselves that we are not alone, to make sense of the world and to see 'how other people do it'. Books give us glimpses, as E.M. Forster remarked, into secret lives.

Reading can also perform the function of healing. Common to every human is the search for belonging, for love, meaning, truth, fulfilment and joy; we all share fears of suffering and death, loneliness, lovelessness and meaninglessness. One of the most fundamental functions of writing as well as reading is to explore, whether in fictional or non-fictional form, some of these issues. Lawrence

Durrell reputedly once suggested that a writer passes a current along a wire, and in so doing frees him- or herself as well as others from doubts and terrors.

An author needs to bear all these possible purposes of literature in mind; a book, no matter how riveting, how wise, will only be as good as its ability to hold the reader's attention, to communicate.

Writers, in a way, straddle the borderlands of the inner world of the imagination and the outer world of experience. If they are able to bring the two together, their creative efforts will not only entertain the reader, but may also have the capacity to uplift, enlighten and transform. Words can change lives.

Once upon a time, art of all kinds was seen as central to the health of both the individual and the culture in which he or she lived. There is undoubtedly a connection between the imagination, and its expression or exercise, and optimum psychological health. 'To awaken the pictures that live in our story-imagination is to become more radiantly and fully alive,' says Nancy Mellon in *Storytelling and the Art of the Imagination*. Native Americans would say that stories are powerful medicine; stories can restore a sense of wellbeing in the listener or reader in a way that little else can. It's no coincidence that some of our myths are hundreds and even thousands of years old. 'Inherent in story is the power to reorder a state of psychological confusion,' says travel writer and essayist Barry Lopez. 'The stories had renewed in me a sense of the purpose of life. This feeling, an inexplicable renewal of enthusiasm after storytelling, is familiar to many people.'

I am, of course, not the first person to remark that we live in strange times. Our society tends to value information, technology and rationality over wisdom, feeling and imagination. Our bias for the last few hundred years has been towards what is known in some circles as the 'left brain' – that is, towards thinking that is rooted in logic, linear processes, analytical understanding and codification. The 'right-brain' values of intuition, imagination, feeling, image-based thought processes and a lateral approach have not been accorded much room or credence. Another way of expressing left and right brain is conscious mind versus unconscious mind. The unconscious part of ourselves is the part that in the past was valued through attention to dream, vision, ritual and religious experience. This is where memories, feelings and imagination abide, and inform the artistic process. This is where stories originate, too. Creative writing is a way of keeping the channels open between this hidden part of ourselves and the conscious mind; good fiction, like good poetry, can open these channels for other people, too, into the rich world of the imagination. A story is like an Ariadne's thread. I've witnessed the power of this over and over in workshops.

Inspired writing which not only makes sense to the head but also comes from and speaks to the heart is a joy both to produce and to read. Writers, I believe, use both the left and right brain if they are writing well. Neither, of course, is complete without the other; both functions need to work in harmony. Your success as a novelist may be rooted in your ability to create original and exciting language – which so often is based on feeling and imagery – but will still depend on finding the appropriate shape for your imaginings. Inspiration and imagination need a structure, a form, if they are to communicate. Your job as a writer is to open the channels, the doors, between the unconscious and the conscious mind, in yourself and for your readers. 'Storytelling,' says Whitbread prizewinner Lindsay Clarke, 'opens a passage from feeling to meaning, converting raw matter to order.'

As a writer and creative writing tutor, I am continually astonished and excited by the power of the imagination. I am constantly looking for new ways of accessing and supporting the creative process and enabling imaginative writing. My background in psychology also reminds me daily of the potency of the unconscious mind and its ability to offer inspiration and wisdom. Over the years in which I have been facilitating workshops I have developed a number of strategies for stimulating creativity in writing. This book combines these with notes for a twenty-week novel-writing course I have been tutoring. It is intended to be a practical book, and intersperses general exercises designed to stimulate the imagination with specific workshop guidelines for writing a novel.

I don't know if creative writing can be taught. Certainly the techniques can be learnt, but the inspirational process itself depends on a number of factors, some of which are unquantifiable (which is appropriate for a right-brain function). There are, however, many ways of enabling the creative process, or at least creating the conditions in which it may take root and bloom. Something happens – factor X – at the point where technique and imagination meet; a kind of alchemy. It's as if the two realms of conscious technique and unconscious imagery meet and create a volatile seam which may suddenly erupt into fire, like flames flaring along a petrol trail.

There are a number of good books available which focus on writing techniques. My aim is not to swell these numbers, but instead to attempt to find ways to redress the balance of which I've been speaking; to help create the conditions for an alchemical encounter to take place. Clearly, the novel-writing core of this book requires an amount of exploration of form and structure. My interest, though, as you will probably have gathered, is in exploring how we can create exciting, impassioned, authentic, vivid language which sings and sparkles and communicates its story effectively.

As readers, we require that a book leaves us in some way changed; if it doesn't, it has perhaps not fulfilled its potential. I hope, in this attempt, to help – if only in a minor way – keep the candles of imagination and inspiration burning in any of you writers who are looking for the most powerful way to communicate your vision to the world. At the very least, I'd like to think that working your way through this book will help you to write a better story.

Roselle Angwin
Dartmoor, June 1998

1 The Creative Writing Process

Living the writer's life

It seems to me that there are two sorts of writers.

The first kind writes purely for their own pleasure, scribbling as and when they feel so inclined. For these 'fair-weather writers' – and I mean no disparagement – the creations of their pens, or keyboards, are their own reward. Writing is a hobby rather than a major motivation, and as such is approached largely with anticipation and delight.

They're the lucky ones.

The second type writes because there is no choice. Writing is an obsession, an addiction, a love-affair, a *raison d'être* which may drive him or her mercilessly, frequently with a fair dose of angst amidst the delight.

Sooner or later this writer will come up against the burning desire to cohabit with this obsession. Spare-time dalliance is no longer enough. The creative form this impulse takes is the 'magnum opus' – usually a novel.

If you have picked up this book, you probably lean, consciously or otherwise, towards the latter category. Perhaps aversion therapy would be more appropriate than a handbook. Writing a novel, if you're serious about it, is a huge commitment, and following the course outlined in this book will involve you in some fairly intense and intensive work. Books like this one should carry a health warning.

Writing any book, but especially a work of the imagination such as a novel, requires that you become single-minded in your focus; that you immerse yourself totally in the world of the imagination and the lives of the characters that you have created. In order to bring the plot and people alive, you have to be prepared to invite this story into your home, share the kitchen, bedroom and bathroom with your characters, climb inside their minds, feel their feelings, act out their fantasies, suffer their tribulations. For the time that you are writing this book, these lives will be as real to you as your own.

In order to avoid being arrested, sectioned or petitioned for divorce, you need to find a way to do all this inside your own head whilst still remembering to eat, relate to your nearest and dearest, get the kids off to school and do the shopping – and probably hold down a job, too. It's like having lodgers, but worse because you are – or should be – emotionally involved with your characters. What's more, you're responsible for their deeds and feelings (if you've had children, you'll understand what I'm talking about). Brace yourself, too, for the sense of bereavement that washes over you when you've finished the writing, when your characters grow up and leave home. The loss is not just limited to that of your characters, either; for after all, where else can you create the perfect life for yourself? It's a shock to come back to what the French call *quotidiennité* – the everyday world and its mundane demands and imperfections.

To the outsider, writing may seem a glamorous occupation. The public face of literature revolves around awards such as the Booker Prize with its prestige and financial rewards, or the book launches with wine and famous names; non-writers imagine a life of divine inspiration punctuated by regular lunches with publishers, agents, film directors and the press.

The reality, of course, is quite different. Writers sweat blood to incubate, deliver and rear their words. Whilst the muse may, if you're lucky, descend with Promethean fire on gilded wings from time to time, most of the writing is sheer hard slog at unsociable hours. Whoever said that writing is 1 per cent inspiration and 99 per cent perspiration was being a little cynical – but only a little. As for wining and dining, many writers work without agents, some never get to meet their publishers, and only a small percentage of books published are given an official launch. And unless you manage to write a bestseller, writing won't make you rich.

Writing is a lonely business. It requires an iron will and strong friendships to resist the temptations of diversions such as evenings out and holidays. It requires sitting down at your desk, whether or not you feel like it. For many writers, the only time available is in the early hours of the morning or late at night. I wrote my first book to its six-month deadline (deadlines are wonderful things) by sitting down at my word processor at ten at night, after my daughter was in bed, having worked all day in the business I was then running. It's crucial that you enjoy solitude – or at least that you are comfortable with it – and that you defend your writing time not only against anyone else who doesn't understand and respect it, but also against your own diversions and displacement activities, inertia, failures of confidence and concerns about selfishness.

The Introduction raised some of the questions surrounding the reasons for reading. So why do we write? The inner compulsion spoken of above takes many forms. For some, the act of writing is cathartic. For others, it's enough to create something, to give it life. Some write to find out what they think, to inform themselves as much as to impart wisdom or information to others. Many write to make sense of their inner world or to find meaning in the outer world, or to find ways of allowing the two to approach each other. Some write because they have a burning need to communicate their vision; others simply to tell a story. It can also be a way of becoming more fully human, developing facets of oneself that have been hidden, giving shape and voice to aspects of the unconscious. We have a whole cast of sub-personalities down there in our depths; while there may not be room for them in our everyday life, we can give them space in our writing, and in doing so discover the treasure-house which lies in our unconscious. But ultimately, most people who write do so because they have to, because not to do so would be in some way a death.

Creativity

Anyone who creates performs a vital function in society. Without wishing to be too precious about it, in a way all artists, including writers, act as messengers, intermediaries between what is and what could be, between everyday life and the life of our dream world, our inner promptings. 'Artists,' says Ben Okri, 'are both shapers and diviners.' Creative inspiration has its genesis in the realms of the gods. In a world dominated by technology, consumerism and a reductionist, materialist viewpoint, creativity and the fire that it keeps alive, in an individual or in a society, has an increasingly crucial value. Adrienne Rich, speaking of the 'fierce charge, or desire' which generates, for instance, a poem, says that this in itself can be a means of saving your life. Whether you're writing fiction, poetry or a journal, the creative flame needs to be honoured, protected and nurtured, and it's a writer's business, right and indeed responsibility to do so. To create is to give life: to inspire, to offer hope, to validate feelings, to give permission, to hold up a mirror, to articulate a vision, to share dreams. Never underestimate the power of language.

There are undoubtedly connections between creativity and wellbeing. Those people who live the most fulfilled lives, actualizing their potential, tend to be the ones who are also the most creative in their approach. It's true that creative types often have more dramatic and extreme lives and experiences than other people. This may, however, not be an expression of neurosis; rather an indication of the values by which they live. Because they are not primarily motivated by the need to feel secure, they are perhaps prepared to take more risks, to extend themselves further. By

Mary Immaculate College
Issue Receipt

Customer name: Sean Kenehan

Title: Creative novel writing
ID: 0101210773
Due: 01/05/2012 21:45

Total items: 1
4/17/2012 11:02 AM

Thank you for using the Self Service System
Please retain this receipt for Due Date

choosing to sail closer to the wind than 'normal' people they open up more of themselves in the process to a wider, deeper experience of the world and themselves.

Words – powerful, dangerous things

Creating something generally involves the manipulation of matter from one form into another. The dynamic relationship between maker and object, if successful, allows a degree of creative participation, however vicarious, on the part of an audience.

The writer, like the musician or composer and to a lesser extent the painter, makes something out of nothing. Words appear out of nowhere and disappear again, leaving a subtly changed universe. (They can, of course, be fixed in a symbolic form on paper, or recorded, to continue to affect all who hear or read them.) This is part of the enchantment of both words and music. Both touch us and move on, leaving us – if they've been successful – changed. But words, language, are primary. 'In the beginning was the word.' The shaping of sounds for the purposes of communication and conveying meaning into the unimaginably immense and sophisticated vocabulary which is the human language is an act of magic that sets us apart from other species.

Words make spells. They have the power to caress, bless, entrance, seduce, excite, hypnotize, terrify, arouse, uplift, punish, condemn. The right word at the right time can transform a situation or an individual in a way that a hundred actions might not.

Words exert control; naming something fixes it, binds it. Their power is recognized: freedom of speech, a basic human right, is rarer than one might think. Historically, and indeed today, certain ways of using words have been outlawed in some places. The Nazis burned books. Salman Rushdie had a *fatwa* put upon him for his perceived attack on Islam in *The Satanic Verses*. Julia Casterton in *Creative Writing* says: 'Books can be dangerous because the reading and writing of them involves us in an exercise of intellectual freedom.' People who think for themselves and encourage others to do so can be a subversive influence.

So words, though they can be used playfully, should never be taken lightly.

The alchemy of words

Writing, says American writer and inspirational tutor Natalie Goldberg, is an act of discovery. She suggests that writers need to cultivate the art of approaching things as if for the first time, each time.

Writing a book is a journey, an adventure. Through writing and through reading we discover and rediscover the world and our relationship to it and with it. A book that is well written, original and imaginative can open doors for its readers to look out on a whole new universe, or to see their familiar universe redefined and become new and inviting. Words in a way reinvent the world. Goldberg says that a writer's job is 'to make the ordinary come alive'; to make the ordinary into the extraordinary. Original writing, in the words of David Lodge, 'by deviating from the conventional habitual ways of representing reality', allows us to perceive the world from a fresh angle, as if for the first time.

You know when you have read good creative writing. This is writing that leaps off the page at you, that hits you in the gut and behind the eyes and in the heart at the same time as imprinting itself in the intellect. This writing ignites something which in turn sets up a reaction in the emotions and in the body. There's a tingle along the spine, the hairs at your neck prickle. This kind of writing is paradoxical: on the one hand, its potency lies in its newness, its freshness, its ability to make us as readers or audience rethink, re-envision our world; simultaneously, it stirs in us the 'Aha!' response which we have when we come across a truth that we have always sensed existed and yet have never seen or heard or articulated. This kind of writing peels back a layer of the world to enable us to look

– really look – at what lies beneath; it offers us glimpses into secret realms, which flesh out the dimensions of our known world as we watch. This is, of course, part of what makes the classics classic.

What does this kind of creativity in writing require?

It needs a cultivated attention to and awareness of the world; the ability to see into the heart of things. It needs a willingness to let go of preconceptions and perceive things as they actually are, moment to moment, with the kind of wonder and curiosity that a child brings to experiences.

It needs a willingness to stalk the wild animals of imagination and inspiration; to learn their territory, watering-holes and habits, to gain their trust.

It requires an originality of theme, or at least an originality of approach to the subject matter.

It takes imaginative and exact use of language, with simultaneously a lateralness and freedom in the choice of vocabulary.

It needs powerful imagery, rooted in the concrete and the natural world.

It requires that for a little time at least the conscious mind stands on one side to allow the unconscious to offer up its fertile territory for investigation. 'The mind should be a cunning net that can catch the fishes of possibility,' says Okri. In the West, we are so concerned with doing that we forget how it is simply to be. With writing, you don't need to actually create the fish; you just need to be in the right place at the right time with your net to hand. The most you often need to do is merely to lift them out and cook them.

Writing is both an active and a passive process. The act of putting words on paper is the active part. The ideas will come of their own accord, once you know how to put yourself in the right place, get out of your own light and watch and wait. Often the most surprising and wonderful insights and imaginings happen when the conscious mind is either engaged in something else or freewheeling. You do not need to force this process, only to learn to make space for it. Part of the purpose of this book is to enable you to find ways to create the right climate for these conditions to flourish. There are exercises in each chapter which, hopefully, will further the creative process in your writing.

It's a bit like harvesting vegetables. All that growing goes on out of sight and largely below ground with minimal help or interference from you, other than the preparation and composting of the soil and the odd bit of judicious watering and weeding. It's quite a miraculous process, the alchemical working of the unconscious mind.

And, most of all, this kind of creativity in writing requires that the writer allows him- or herself to feel the full range of human emotions. Unless he or she is able to do this, the resultant writing will remain pale and unconvincing. To engage your reader you need to be able to imagine and articulate the whole spectrum of human experience.

Taking risks

'Living is a form of not being sure, not knowing what next or how. The moment you know how, you begin to die a little. The artist never entirely knows. We guess. We may be wrong, but we take leap after leap in the dark.' (Agnes de Mille)

If you want to write you need to be able to take risks – in your life and in your writing. If you only want to stay where you are, safe and secure, then you will only ever be a mediocre writer. You have to be prepared to stretch yourself; to look into the dark places, to be moved to tears and laughter, to be honest and truthful, to write about your anger, your pain, your memories, your fear, as well as your loves, your joys, your triumphs. Not that these things will necessarily go into your novels; merely that you'll be writing from a superficial place if you're not prepared to fully experience life and write from the depths of that experience. How can you write about falling in love, or the death of a child, or betrayal, or a car accident, or transformation, without at least being prepared to imagine how it would feel to experience these things?

And don't be afraid to get it wrong. Jazz saxophonist Coleman Hawkins reputedly said: 'If you don't make mistakes, you aren't really trying'.

There are times in one's writing, as in one's life, when the only thing you can do is jump, often with no idea of where you will land. There are no guarantees; and trying to find lasting security will only result in a deadening as you close yourself down tighter and tighter. With practice, you can learn to trust your impulses, your intuition, your imagination; the unconscious can generally be relied upon to come up with what it is you need. So trust yourself to take creative risks.

In the words of Brenda Ueland: 'Be bold, be free, be truthful.'

Imagination and the unconscious

I suggested in the Introduction that the creative self may be found in the borderlands between the unconscious realm of the intuitive imagination and the conscious realm of learned technique. A friend and colleague, the editor Richard Beaumont, says that for him writing is a fine balance between possession and objectivity. This, I think, sums it up. So words of imagination spring from an encounter between the emotional, image-based, lateral, instinctual right brain and the shaping ordering function of the logical, literal left brain. I also said that in the West we tend to overemphasize the latter and undervalue the former, thus cutting ourselves off to a large extent from the wisdom of the unconscious.

I'd like to look briefly here at ways of reconnecting with the unconscious.

Ted Hughes, in his foreword to a book by John Fairfax and John Moat (*The Way To Write*) and talking about the Arvon writing courses, says that when a writing student is put in possession of 'the creative self', two things in particular become much more interesting: the working of language and the use of literature. The discovery or rediscovery of the creative self 'brings about . . . in an organic and natural way, what years of orthodox English teaching almost inevitably fail to bring about except in the most artificial and external way'. Hughes goes on to say that a student is awakened to a new awareness of the real life of language, with all its dynamic power. Literature, he says, is then seen for what it is – a living organism conveying 'the psychological record of this drama of being alive', articulating and illuminating all the depth and breadth and subtlety of being human.

How we can meet the requirements of this creative self and find effective channels for its expression is the fundamental theme of this book.

Learning to pay attention to the creative promptings of the unconscious is an important first step. Robert Johnson, in *Inner Work*, suggests that there are two natural pathways for bridging the gap between the worlds of the unconscious and conscious mind. One is by *dreams*, the other is through the *imagination*.

Dreams

If you are not already in the habit of paying attention to your dreams, I strongly recommend that you start. Apart from their psychological usefulness in highlighting areas of your life which are calling for attention, they have a rôle to play in expanding the field of possibilities for nourishing your creative self. Get into the habit of recording them as soon as you wake in the morning. This serves a triple purpose: acknowledging the presence of the unconscious; opening a dialogue; and accustoming you to the natural language of the unconscious – symbols, feelings, moods. You may find as a bonus that scenes, situations and images from your dream world provide the raw material for later imaginative work. Whether this happens or not, recording your dreams in writing helps to keep the doors open.

Imagination

There is part of us that is hungry for flights of the imagination, to be free of the constraints of ego, logic and everyday concerns, to enter new realms and be shown new possibilities, other ways of living. Imagination, says Lindsay Clarke, is the connection between the individual and *anima mundi*, the soul of the world. Imagination *animates*.

Johnson says: 'Humans depend on the imagination's image-making power and its image-symbols for poetic imagery, literature, painting, sculpture, and essentially all artistic, philosophical and religious functioning.' He goes on to say that it's inconceivable that we could develop 'abstract intelligence, science, mathematics, logical reasoning, or even language' had we not the capacity to generate these image-symbols.

The imagination as an organ of communication, says Johnson, employs a highly refined, complex language of symbols to convey the promptings of the unconscious via images that are received by the conscious mind.

Learn to pay attention to this language. Take notice of your daydreams, fantasies, feelings and moods as well as spontaneous images and those little voices which whisper extraordinary ideas into your mind at the seemingly most inappropriate moments.

How else can we feed or free our imaginations?

- by steeping ourselves in art, music, theatre and film
- by listing all the places, situations or events which inspire us and then committing ourselves to making regular time for them
- by learning new creative skills such as playing an instrument, painting, pottery or sculpture
- by spending time with stimulating people
- by learning to think laterally (see workshop suggestions at the end of this chapter)

Ideas both feed and free this process. It goes without saying, I hope, that writers need also to be readers. Good literature and inspiring ideas speak to our imaginations. An idea is a living thing.

The unconscious – and its imaginative processes – enjoys playing. Have fun while you're doing all this. To start you off, here are a couple of word-games to encourage you to think laterally and give your imagination a treat. You can do them alone, but it's more stimulating, and enjoyable, to play them with others.

Writing practice

The first game was inspired by the hilariously wonderful *Meaning of Liff* by Douglas Adams and John Lloyd.

Take a place-name – any name, from anywhere. What might it mean? For instance (from the book):

COTTERSTOCK (n.): A piece of wood used to stir paint and thereafter stored uselessly in a shed in perpetuity.

HEANTON PUNCHARDON (n.): A violent argument which breaks out in the car on the way home from a party between a couple who have had to be polite to each other in company all evening.

LULWORTH (n.): Measure of conversation. A lulworth defines the amount of the length, loudness and embarrassment of a statement you make when everyone else in the room unaccountably stops talking at once.

The second game is Dictionary (this is also available in commercial card-game form as Chicanery). This one's best played with others, and you might wish to devise a scoring system.

Take a number of obscure words from a dictionary, along with their definitions (you'll need either enough dictionaries to go around, or enough time and patience to await your turn). Each person or team works with a different word. Don't share the original meaning of the word with anyone else except a team-mate if you're working in teams. Now make up a number of alternative definitions for these words – perhaps four. The idea is to read out these definitions along with the correct one for the other players to try and guess which is the original dictionary definition.

One way of scoring is for the author(s) to score a point for each definition of their own picked as the correct one, whilst the opposing (guessing) team gains a point if they guess correctly.

Here are some examples:

UMIAK

1 Name given to large Himalayan hairy horned beast by first Englishman to encounter it
2 An archaic word meaning butter churn
3 Indian name for falconer's hunting jesses
4 An open boat paddled by Eskimo women
5 An Eastern European prototype car
6 Floating jetsam found under iceberg
7 Turkish souk storeholder's hidden money-bag

(Number 4 is the dictionary definition.)

ULOTRICHOUS

1 Heavenly merit achieved on chanting after the Russian Orthodox equivalent of confession
2 Having one nostril more prominent than the other
3 Being verbally abusive in a public place
4 Inclined to romantic entanglement, extra-marital or otherwise
5 Having tightly-curled hair

(Number 5 is correct.)

Some words to start you off: STOICHOMETRY, ODON-TOGLOSSUM, LIGROIN, DARIOLE, COLURE, CASUIST, ALIQUOT and TURBARY.

2 Writing it Down

Making space

Most writers cannot afford the luxury of an office or studio away from the house, but it's hard working from home; there are too many distractions. It's a funny thing, but friends and family quite inadvertently view your working from home in a way that they wouldn't if you were working in an office elsewhere all day. It doesn't help, either, if you have to keep clearing your writing off the kitchen table to make way for domestic needs.

A corner which you can call your own is crucial. So if you can, set up a desk somewhere which you use exclusively for writing, and on which you can leave your papers undisturbed. It's much easier to get down to work if it's there waiting for you than if you have to go through the rigmarole of clearing a table, amassing your papers, research material or notes and finding your place before you can think about starting. For many people, the bedroom is the only available space, but this is not ideal, as the subconscious message then is that the bedroom is for working, and your brain may start to switch on each time you enter the room, even when the message should be to relax and sleep.

As important as the physical space is your attitude to your writing and the area in which you do it. If you can, put your desk near a window; whether you are able to or not, ensure that the light is good. It also helps if you make your workspace inviting, with fresh flowers, an inspiring picture or quotes from other writers. Your subconscious needs to know that you take this work seriously and are going to give it your best efforts.

In terms of commitment, what you are writing is, initially at least, of less importance than the act of writing itself. ('One story or poem doesn't matter one way or the other. It's the process of writing and life that matters . . . if the process is good, the end will be good,' says Natalie Goldberg.) Whatever your literary focus, make a pact with yourself that you will write for, say, a minimum of half an hour each weekday, or whatever works for you. If you need to get up half an hour earlier in order to do this, so be it. I warned you that the writer's life wasn't all honey and roses. It's a myth that writers write only as and when the muse takes them. If this were so, there would be far fewer books in the world, and virtually no newspapers or magazines. Having said that, because the emphasis in this book is on the creative imagination, one has to ask whether the world might be a better place if there were fewer publications of the pedestrian, unoriginal and frankly dull and uninspired variety. How to avoid falling into that trap is part of the purpose of this book.

For myself, I write poetry as and when the muse appears. I write fiction and non-fiction, however, just about every day, regardless of inspiration or otherwise, though undoubtedly my work is better when there is a modicum of inspiration behind it.

Before we move on, it's perhaps important to reiterate that making space for writing in your life is not just about snatching a moment and cramming a desk into a spare corner. It's about allowing a sense of spaciousness into your interior life, too, so that the flame may be lit and will have enough oxygen to glow brightly and gain strength. This needs practice and a certain amount of mindfulness; a writer needs to learn how to shut out the outside world and its demands and false busyness and turn inwards, towards the imaginative life.

Getting started

All you need for writing in principle, of course, is a notebook and pen. You can write anywhere – on the train, on holiday, in the bath, in your lunch break. Compulsive writers do. Certainly it's important to carry a notebook with you wherever you go; for ideas, snippets of conversations, quotes, inspiring poems, records of the way winter sunlight falls across the fields or on puddles, the exact shade of blue of someone's scarf, the texture of a satsuma as you peel it and its taste on your tongue. This is the stuff of which books are made, eventually.

A common question from beginning writers is: do I need a typewriter or word processor? To which, I'm sorry to say, the answer is yes; at least if you're writing for publication. You may prefer to write first drafts in longhand; that's fine. Bear in mind, however, that there's scarcely an editor or publisher who will even bother to glance at a manuscript written in longhand; it smacks of the amateur, and if you don't take yourself seriously, why should they? Then there's the expense of finding someone to type up your finished work – always assuming they can read your writing – which may amount to almost the same cost as buying a basic word processor. Word processors are user-friendly on the whole, and soon become addictive. If you're the kind of writer who doesn't know what they want to say until they've written it, they're invaluable, as you can move whole chunks of writing around at will without having to cross out, drain the correction fluid or retype.

It really helps to have goals and to establish a writing routine; but make your targets achievable so that you feel good about what you're doing rather than guilty if you fail.

Notice which time of day is your most creative, intellectually vigorous time, and if you can rearrange other aspects of your life to accommodate your writing at this time, do so. Incidentally, burning essential oil of rosemary in your workroom can help sharpen your mental processes, and there are other oils, such as sandalwood and frankincense and some of the flower oils, which seem to ease one's passage into the world of the imagination.

There are days when the writing flows and you write a couple of thousand words before breakfast without even noticing. Often, though, your designated half hour (or whatever) will be gone in a flash with little to show for it. This is how it is; life is all ebb and flow and it's pointless despairing. The very act of sitting down at your desk at around the same time each day is in itself the best start that a writer can make on any creative project. On the days when the flow seems to have ebbed, sit down, pick up your pen or switch on your word processor and just write. Act 'as if'. Don't worry about what you're writing, just get some words down. You can always scrub them or bin them; but in the process of just writing, many people find they stumble upon what they want to say. It's a bit like the seventh sister of the Pleiades: you can see her best by focusing on something else to one side of her. You can trick or surprise the subconscious – or perhaps vice versa. To mix a metaphor, the act of merely opening the channels by writing something – anything – can yield a seam of gold.

There will be days when you don't know how to continue with your novel; sit down as usual and write something else instead. Later in this chapter are some suggestions for writing topics to keep your creative muscles stretched even when the novel seems to have ground temporarily to a halt. Bear in mind, too, that time spent thinking about your work, making notes and doing research is still working time – but try not to use it to procrastinate.

Writer's block and other diversions

I'm not sure I believe in writer's block. It's a luxury a professional writer can't afford, and it's amazing how something akin to block disappears as a deadline rushes nearer! The easiest cure I find, as I've already says, is to switch on the word processor. Of course there are times when your writing feels clumsy, dull and uninspired, just as there are times when you'd much rather watch television or go to the pub than write. These two things are, I suspect, at the bottom of what people call writer's block.

It's amazing what you can find to use as a diversion. Six days out of seven you may not even notice the dust in the house, let alone do anything about it. But as soon as you're just a little anxious about something you're in the middle of writing, cleaning the house or washing the dishes seems to be of paramount importance. And then it's time for another cup of coffee, and there's a phone call you ought to make . . . and maybe you'll just walk up to the postbox with that letter that's been hanging around for several days . . .

At times like this the following strategies may help:

- First, check whether you're just avoiding the discipline of writing or whether you've become stale. It's necessary to the writing process to allow the well to fill up again, as Hemingway described it. Your ideas need the mental equivalent of frequent fresh air. If you know that you're feeling empty, drained, determinedly turn your face away from your book and do something *practical*. For some, going for a walk always recharges their imaginative batteries. Chopping wood or gardening may help, or baking bread, making a cake, playing with children, clearing out a cupboard, going to a film or a concert. (Yes, I know I said beware of distractions. Just be aware of why you're choosing to do this: because your unconscious needs it, or because you've got to a sticky bit.) The more you occupy your conscious mind, the more the unconscious will beaver away for you. Keep your notebook to hand; your best ideas will come dancing in at the most inopportune moments: in the supermarket or when driving, in a meeting, in the middle of the night.
- Try and pace yourself. Hemingway's method of working, apparently, was to make himself stop writing around midday, even though he knew (or perhaps especially because he knew) what needed to be written next. It's said that he then occupied his time by being out in the garden, tending his beehives. He wouldn't allow himself to continue writing then until early the next day.

When training a young horse, there's a basic principle which a sympathetic trainer follows: to stop on a high note, when the horse is eager and keen to continue. The temptation as a writer is to write until the flow dries up; it may be more helpful, psychologically, to stop before this, so that you already know what you're going to say before you sit down again to continue.

- Kickstart your imagination by reading poetry or listening to music or going around an art gallery. Many people find that writing to classical music stimulates their imagination. If you have a regular meditation practice, this can help your writing tremendously. Active visualizations – guided meditations – are extremely helpful to a writer, both for direct inspiration and to help the well fill up. There is more about these in chapter five. It may be worth using a tape (see 'Useful Addresses').

- As I've already said, sit at your desk and write anyway; anything that comes to mind.

- Forget your novel for a few days but commit yourself to writing something every day for fifteen minutes. Try a 'stream-of-consciousness' as soon as you wake up (of which more later). This has three effects: you feel better for continuing to write; this in itself can loosen up your imaginative/mental muscles; and quite often you can dig up a nugget of gold this way if you don't think too hard about it.

- If none of these work for you, backtrack. You may need to think about what you're trying to do with the book. Are you happy about the storyline, clear about the plot, beginning, major turning points and ending? Has the middle gone soggy and do you need to inject something else to maintain suspense? Do you have the right central character and is he-she clear in your mind? Have you started at the right point? Are you resisting rewriting something that needs it? Are you just plain bored with what you're writing? Make notes, reassess what you're doing. Remind yourself what the central theme of the book is.

- Be ruthless with yourself. Are you scared, lazy, and avoiding or resisting the discipline of sitting down, thinking and writing? Anxious that you can't do it? Believe in yourself. Everyone feels like this at times, especially with creative work. Courage!

Good writing habits

There are writers who, while writing a major work, deliberately avoid reading anything by anyone else. I understand the admirable reasons behind this: that they don't wish to be influenced by other writers and/or risk plagiarism. However, I don't believe that any creative work ever arises in a vacuum. We are to a large extent what our experiences have made us, and this will include the hundreds of thousands of books we may have read in our lifetime, as well as all the ideas and philosophies we have absorbed. It's impossible to avoid influence completely, and on the whole plagiarism is unconscious in any case. There are only so many original themes in the world; what matters in literature is how well you make your subject your own, and then how well you express it.

Almost without exception, good writers are also avid readers. How can you expect to be able to judge the quality of your own work, let alone know whether it's publishable or not, unless you are able to recognize other people's talent? You need to be able not only to see what's being published, but also to recognize what makes the greats, the established and the contemporary classics, what they are. And the only way to do this is to read and read and read. If you do not have the kind of voracious appetite for words that involves reading even the cornflakes packet at breakfast, cultivate it. Whilst it's important to learn discrimination, it's also important to explore as wide a range of genres and writing styles as possible. I'm not asking you necessarily to assess and analyse the books you read, but it may be helpful to keep in mind the question: does this book offer me insights, enable me to look at things with a fresh eye, challenge my views of reality, engage me, deepen my understanding? You may find that as you sink deeper into your own writing, you will have an increased tendency to read books bifocally: on one level for entertainment, information, pleasure, insight or whatever your personal reasons for reading are, and on another level for the author's handling of the intricacies of plotting, style, characterization, dialogue and so forth.

All of this will ensure that you have a clearer, truer ear for recognizing your own voice.

So good writing habit number one is to read.

Equally important is to keep writing. Yes, I know you're writing a novel. It's not enough. If you were dancing *Swan Lake* you wouldn't expect to just get up on stage each night and suddenly be foot-perfect. You would do your warm-up exercises and then practise, practise, practise, over and over, day after day. 'Don't stop doing writing practice just because you're writing a novel,' says Goldberg. Writing practice, she says, is 'our wild forest where we gather energy before going to prune our garden, write our fine books and novels'.

Writing practise is the literary equivalent of playing scales.

Each person will have his or her own method of approach. I strongly suggest, though, that you develop a habit of writing in a free, uncensored way for ten to fifteen minutes of each day. The work that you produce here is not intended for public consumption, but purely to 'open the channels' between the conscious and the unconscious. (Having said that, some of the most powerful, moving writing from students in workshops has been this 'warm-up' writing.) To some extent, this is intended to be 'automatic writing' in the sense that you are leaving on one side considerations to do with content, making sense, syntax, punctuation and grammar – everything to do with shaping and structuring. Tidy writing is not what this work is about. Rather it's about giving free rein to our spontaneous inner emotional and imaginative processes – about which more later.

There are various different ways of doing this. You can write to music. You could take a line (or a phrase or a word or image) from a poem and follow that thread. You can use a word or a topic from the list given later in this chapter or devise one of your own. Try writing with your unaccustomed hand. Or you can just write.

Stream-of-consciousness writing

James Joyce and Virginia Woolf are often quoted as typifying 'stream-of-consciousness' writing. To my mind, their work sits halfway between what I think of as true stream-of-consciousness and structured writing – inevitably, perhaps, as their books are intended both to be read and to convey some sort of narrative, albeit highly individual.

The term is a bit of a misnomer, as actually what I'm talking about is stream-of-*un*consciousness. It's rather like a painter assembling a palette of experimental colours. This kind of 'freeflow' writing is particularly effective if you can write the moment you wake up, before a cup of tea, before anything; certainly before the day cuts in with its demands. At this time you are closer to the unconscious and its world of dreams and images, memories and feelings, and your writing will reflect this. You can do it anywhere, though – on a bus, in a café – just filling pages. Eventually you'll become reasonably adept at switching off the 'left-brain' logical, critical function and this practice can become like a meditation. Think of your writing hand as being an unquestioning camera, recording unconditionally whatever registers on the surface of your mind.

Don't expect – don't look for – dazzling writing. There may be some, but that's not the point. To start with you'll probably find yourself just writing stilted froth, regurgitated dross, day-to-day occurrences, thoughts, events. It's very hard to let go of tidy-mind consciousness, too; many people find this kind of writing difficult initially. Eventually, though, you'll cut through the superficialities and move below the surface and start discovering what you really want to say. This practice can become very important, and you may find yourself writing with unexpected vigour, colour and insight; and almost certainly you will find that the calibre of your 'proper' writing will take a quantum leap.

This is different from the usual journal-writing in that it is not intended to be merely a record of events or thoughts or feelings. It's intended to be a net in which you can 'catch the fishes of possibility' – which may include all of those things. You're dropping a berry on a thread, in the words of W.B. Yeats, into the pool of the subconscious and lifting whatever is there, ready to emerge.

There are some guidelines. First, don't *think*. This is extraordinarily hard, as all our educative processes are about just this. Thinking is a linear progression; the type of writing we're exploring here is more akin to a mosaic or a collage of word-pictures, lateral and not necessarily obviously linked one to the other. So leave the need to make sense outside the door when you do this. Allow images, feelings and memories to arise spontaneously and immediately and without thought note them down – this is the natural language of the subconscious.

Secondly, allow yourself to be a passenger rather than a driver. Follow the thread, wherever it leads you, however bizarre or unexpected the ideas. Allow your mind to jump around, make crazy connections, run where it will. Allow word-association to guide you. This is free time, off-the-lead time.

Thirdly, try not to be afraid of the darker images which may at times arise. If you feel sad or angry, write about it.

Fourthly and most importantly, once you've started don't stop writing until the time is up, and don't read your work back until you've finished. Keep the pen moving over the paper, writing down anything that comes into your head. If you get stuck, just write, 'I am stuck I am stuck I am stuck' until your hand comes up with something else to write, or go back to your opening phrase and see where it leads you this time. Follow it, trust it.

Perhaps it's important to add: don't judge your writing. Put it away and don't read it again for some days or even weeks.

Possible topics for writing practice

Sun, ice, fire, flint, crossing the border, bone, loss, holiday, dying, I remember, my mother says, attic, threshold, when it was over, once, stone, water, bread, on the train, corridor, first kiss, leaving, cave, church, cellar, orchard, in the garden, the last time, party . . . the list can, of course, go on *ad infinitum*. Make your own list for the times when you run short of ideas; choose ones to which you have some kind of feeling response. For this kind of writing you might like to use scrap paper or a recycled spiral-bound notebook. If you use good paper you might feel too inhibited to allow yourself to write whatever comes, because you can be sure that some of it at least will be rubbish (probably). Keep these exercises; apart from their interest value as a record of your inner life, you might like to look back and see how far you've come in terms of letting yourself free-wheel, and in originality of language, after a few months. And there's also the odd phrase which you might want to lift and use in something else, or as a starting point.

Examples

These are all stream-of-consciousness pieces written to a time-limit: the first one five minutes, the others three minutes each. None of them has been edited or revised. The first two pieces used lines from other people's work as starting points.

The first one took 'silence inside this circle of sound' from a poem by Gillian Clarke.

> Silence inside this circle of sound
> outside, the petulant wind, flinging rain like gravel against the window, sending squalls shrieking and wheezing down the chimney – brief flowers of steam bursting like gunshot from amongst these cinders
> silence inside this circle of sound
> the candle wavers and flickers, strengthens again, burns brightly even though you are not here
> in the meadow the horses will be huddled under trees already stripped, rags of leaves skimming like flights of birds over their rumps, dreadlock tails flicking wet backs, rosettes of shorter hairs splayed muddy
> in the garden the tree is bare of fruit, one moulding apple perhaps succumbing to the relentless lips of slugs – or do they have teeth – gums – over the roar of the storm I imagine I hear the munching

slobber – strange, slugs having mouths
the garden is a mouth, and the night
the dog is buried under the apple tree. I was digging the pit the day
R.'s bombshell letter arrived with the jolly whistling postman. The
ground was icebound – even the laurels frozen – and Christmas
might as well have been a foreign language
his card with its false cheer, tacky glitter
that mouth nearly swallowed me up; I nearly fell, kept falling, falling
into dark
'Mummy please don't let them bury me alive'
lighting a candle
you are not here
silence inside this circle of sound where I sit, stripped naked of
summer like the apple tree, awaiting winter

You can see that this is not great literature (the best bit is the start-ing line!), but the images conjure other images and old memories. I like the picture of the slobbering slugs, steadily focused on their own appetites irrespective of anything else, and the hissing rain-drops making 'brief flowers of steam bursting like gunshot from amongst these cinders', and the idea of the night as a mouth. This was my own piece; I've underlined the phrases I liked in my orig-inal copy in case I find a use for them some time.

Inspired by the same poem but using a different line as a start-ing point ('chalking the slate floor') is a piece by a student, Chris Tooke:

Chalking the slate floor with stones dust from the woodworm shaking like pepper onto the polished floor hinting no warning like a clanging bell of the danger one little beetle can wreak I think it's a beetle that lays its eggs which hatch into worms that thread them-selves into the panel churning along the gullies indiscriminate making paths like feet through grassland or layers of leaves in a wood this wood built around you your own little fortress waiting to crumble at the threat of a beetle

The next piece, again by Chris Tooke, comes from a phrase given out in a workshop: 'when it was over'.

When it was over the deadly silence whistled through my head lines on the wire fence whispered like a current bent on your last word sly crusty word hard line on winter pelts of fur hung on the line like whispers tails hanging wet matted dung clinging on hindquarters like slime on a stick run through a stream lights flickered on the back wall lighting up the fallen stone the crevices filled with black spider eggs until a million tiny forms crawled along the hedge light catching brushing the jet of movement that clung in silvered lines on crumbling stone eyes on furrows whistling in droves and cream silk shadows draped webs taut between the doors and window frames like gossamer curtains flicked open with a tiny draught of air you were the whisper that called me back line upon line of fresh blowing thread your voice on a back burner waiting to be heard and recalled on some winter morning a flash of memory unasked for but suddenly there acute

Chris has a natural feel for imagery. Here she juxtaposes gentle poetic images – cream silk shadows, gossamer curtains – with more savage somewhat menacing images like the deadly silence, hanging pelts of fur and the black spider eggs, hooking my feelings. Her metaphors hint at the now-light, now-dark nature of human relationships. She draws a reader in, too, with the repetition of words and ideas.

The next piece is also by Chris. Here she wrote from her own images rather than using a phrase as a starting point; immediately prior to the writing I had read the group a number of poems by T.S. Eliot.

Reflect my hand in your hand against a bed of feathers and circled around your head a halo light from the window caught on the goosedown yellow from the picture frame holding your grandparents circled in gilt edged history warm reflection from their strange still faces upright figures looking down on your twisted yet relaxed frame lying as though waiting for something to happen eyes half closed against the thin shard of sunlight we cannot block out a sheet of thin Indian cotton transparent to your charms ice melting on warm thighs fold lines cast around your heart as though protecting that little piece you will not show me though sometimes I can feel its glow

Finally a piece using a phrase of Ben Okri's to start: 'there is a red wind in my head'.

There's a red wind in my head he said today and nothing I can do to brush it out It's like the desert came and walked all over trailing bits of itself across our days There's a red wind in my head and in my hair like wild catprints rattlesnake tracks thorny desert claws camel spoor The red wind shouts. I want – I want a paintbrush slosh it all over blue slow it down a bit lick spit stick it back where it belongs inside some book, inside some map Shut it There's a red wind in my head and all I see is blood today he said

Writing practice

Stream-of-consciousness

Give yourself a few minutes to scan through a book of poems or a novel until you find a phrase that inspires you. Shut yourself away somewhere quiet and jot down the phrase. Time yourself – set an alarm, perhaps; maybe three to five minutes for a first time – and following the guidelines above start writing and keep writing until the time is up.

Focusing – your novel

If you've already started writing your novel you'll have some kind of working method set up, though you'll probably benefit from what I'm about to suggest.

Buy yourself a notebook for writing practice. In addition to this, buy a large ring-binder file and some file dividers. Mark the file with your working title (if you don't have one, make one up now; it doesn't have to be the final choice, but once more it will help you to take your writing seriously).

Make the first section the one where you keep all the exercises relating to working through this book but not directly connected with the novel. (These are different from writing practice work.)

Your second section will be details of plot, blurb, synopsis and so forth.

The third section will be your list of chapters. Take four or five sheets of A4 paper, and allowing a quarter or half a page per chapter, write the numbers in the margin: 1–12 or so. If you know what your beginning and ending are going to be, and roughly where the major scenes come, pencil them in accordingly (you can always swop them around later). This will start to give you a feel for the shape of the book; you'll probably find this immensely helpful. As you write each chapter, whether or not you write them sequentially, keep details on these sheets of the main events and characters in this chapter, their ages, physical appearance at the time of writing, location etc.

The fourth section is your character-portrait section, and the fifth will be for general notes, ideas and brief scenes which have yet to find their right place in the book. The final section will be for the actual novel.

Your first exercise (for the first section of your folder) is brief. Question yourself as follows, set yourself goals and note this all down.

1 List all the kinds of books you tend to read.
2 Describe in general terms the kind of book you'd most like to write, in fifty words.
3 What would you like to have achieved by the end of this book?

The obvious answer, of course, is to be well on the way to completing a novel. There are other possibilities, though:

- to take yourself seriously as a writer
- to have been writing daily
- to have developed your creative and imaginative powers
- to have dreamt up the plot for a second book

4 Why do you read novels?
5 Why do you want to write one? (Be honest!)
6 How much writing time are you going to try to commit to the novel each day/week?
7 How are you going to go about writing practice?

These may all seem to be trivial questions, but they serve to focus your intent and the act of writing down the answers is a message to your subconscious of this intent. Do it now, before you read on and before your good intentions get swept away.

3 Starting the Novel

Secret Lives

A significant function of the novel is the privileged access we gain, as E.M. Forster pointed out in *Aspects of the Novel*, into the secret interior of the characters portrayed. If the characters are well portrayed, we are able to lose ourselves, and the concerns of our own lives, in the life of someone else in a way that is rare in 'real' life. How hard it is to truly understand another, remarked Forster, to reveal ourselves even when we really want to, to enter into someone else's life. Intimacy, he says, is 'a makeshift'; perfect intimacy, it seems, an impossibility. In the novel, however, we can enter the life of another fully.

What's more, we can remake history. Fiction goes beyond the mere statement of fact, the cataloguing of events, and allows us to imagine the normally invisible human aspects: the emotions, reactions, thoughts and imaginings of the characters. Where the historian records, the novelist creates. The chronicle of events in a person's life, made up of observable actions and spoken thoughts, what we could call his or her history, is the aspect which we most commonly share, with glimpses now and then of what makes the person 'tick'. The other, more hidden side of a person's life, that which is made up of 'pure passions, dreams, joys, sorrows and self-communings', along with fantasies, imaginings, visions or spiritual aspirations, doubts and fears, which 'politeness or shame prevent him from mentioning' we can only imagine, unless the other person chooses to share them with us. A novel can and should portray both the 'surface' life of a character, and the inner life. The expression of this other side of human nature is perhaps a novel's strength and major attraction.

Forster makes much of the fact that the speciality of the novel is this glimpse into private lives: 'The novelist can talk about his characters as well as through them; or can arrange for us to listen when they talk to themselves . . . He can descend and peer into the subconscious [of the character]', laying it all bare for us to witness. The novelist, of course, manipulates the characters, the story, and also the audience, according to what he or she wishes to convey, to achieve.

Characters and plots

What do you wish to convey? What story are you wanting to tell? Why? It helps to be clear about all this from the start. If you can remain focused on your storyline and your intention in telling the story it will add to the coherence and the cohesiveness of your novel.

A decision you will need to make early on – if it's not already been decided by the nature of the book – is whether your interest is largely in development of plot or development of character.

While all, or certainly most, novels of course contain both characters and plot, there are nonetheless two distinct types: those which are action-driven, where the plot is the most important thing, and those which are character-driven. So the focus is different. In an action-driven book, the characters exist largely as tools to develop the action, and they tend, to a greater or lesser extent and perhaps necessarily, to fall into recognizable stereotypes. Because the thrust of the book is the resolution of the plot, the characters will not necessarily be changed by events. In a character-driven book, the plot acts as a vehicle for the characters to develop, change and grow, and it is not so important that the book is gripping and dramatic.

So we have two strands, one of which is normally subservient to the other. Ronald Tobias in *Twenty Master Plots and How to Build Them*, defines them thus:

- the pattern of plot, where the dynamic force of the storyline will guide you through the action
- the pattern of character, where the actors in the plot provide a dynamic force of behaviour that will guide you through your characters' intent and motivation.

Bearing in mind that in actuality these strands are not separated quite as clearly as I've just described, which interests you most, action or psychology? Until you have gained experience in both approaches, you may be best initially following your natural inclinations.

Each has its own dangers. If the book is all action, it's easy for the characters to become too flat, too stereotypical – puppets whose actions are superficial and not always credible in terms of real people. However, as long as the plot is sufficiently imaginative and suspenseful, readers can be persuaded to suspend their disbelief.

If the book is wrapped up in the psychology of the characters, the danger is that it becomes merely an exposition of navel-gazing intensity, or simply a series of minor incidents seemingly unconnected and rambling, with no strong storyline.

The writing of the novel, whatever its emphasis, of course, requires the same overall approach, as the guidelines apply to both; one instance is the need to generate tension. Whether your book is plot- or character-driven, the development of the story is likely, as an example, to require that your main character finds her-himself at least once, and probably more often, between a rock and a hard place. Both styles depend on the novelist's ability to set up a situation, generate tension, and offer some kind of resolution.

A good novelist, clearly, will pay attention to both plot and character development, whilst managing to keep the writing uncluttered. It is usually discernible, however, which is the important factor for any given novelist. Getting the balance right between weight of plot and weight of character means that inevitably one or other of them occasionally suffers. Becoming aware of when and how this happens will enable you to make adjustments.

'Genre' or 'contemporary' novel?

It's probably true to say that the 'genre' novels such as sci-fi, fantasy, horror, crime, historical, westerns and romance, are on the whole plot-driven. Contemporary and literary novels tend to lean the other way, although they will have elements of one or several genres in their structure.

Whilst there will probably always be a market for the plot-driven book, a glance at the shelves in any major bookstore will show the increased popularity of books where character-portrayal is paramount. There has been a shift in the reading public's tastes over the last ten or twenty years, away from genre novels and towards what is loosely described as the 'contemporary' novel, which has at its core the interactions and complexities of human relationship in all its shapes and forms, whether that relationship is to other people, to the wider world or to oneself – usually all three.

The major difference is in the emphasis, and perhaps also the purpose. A detective story, for instance, or the novels of say Dick Francis or Mary Stewart, may be intended primarily as 'a good read', gripping readers right up until the last page. We are less concerned with the characters themselves than with their position in relationship to the plot. They are vehicles. We expect to see the story resolved, and we are likely to remember the book because we remember the plot.

On the other hand a novel such as Lindsay Clarke's *Alice's Masque* explores the nature of male/female relationships as well as the mysteries and phenomena of the natural world, and is concerned with the growth and transformation of the central character. The questions raised about the nature of the world and our relation to it, and our empathy or otherwise with the characters – in other words the feeling tone and the philosophical undercurrents – may be what stay in our mind afterwards. In this case, the plot is a vehicle for the exploration of character and idea. The contemporary novel with literary overtones tends to concern itself with one or two strong characters attempting to make their place in the world. D.H. Lawrence was an exponent of this, as are Iris Murdoch, Helen Dunmore and A.S. Byatt, perhaps also Julian Barnes.

Having said all that, the categories are clearly less well defined than I have portrayed them here. How would you categorize the novels of Jane Austen and the Brontës, or Thomas Hardy? Many modern novelists have a foot in both camps. Joanna Trollope is one; maybe Jane Smiley and John Fowles. Where do you put *The English Patient* as a book, and as a film – and *The Horse Whisperer*? Popular novelist Dorothy Dunnett recreates the historical world through an adventure story and a plethora of colourful characters, and while her books do not pretend to be about the world of ideas and possibilities, her skilful handling of both plot and characterization, as well as her formidable historical knowledge, allows us to feel we are involved in the life of the characters.

There are also, novels which refuse to be categorized according to the usual conceptions; Jeanette Winterson's work is an example of this. These more experimental novels are largely outside the scope of this book.

What is of importance in exploring ways of writing a novel is that if you choose to break the rules, you should do it consciously and deliberately, which of course means knowing what the rules are in the first place. As in any artistic discipline – dance, painting, music, photography, poetry – the best exponents are often those who have the classical training to be able to choose what to keep and what to jettison. The purpose of this book is to equip you to make some of these choices as informed decisions. (The danger, of course, is the formulaic repetition of a set of rules: writing by numbers.)

Whose story?

It's important, too, to know from the outset through whose eyes you wish to follow the story. We'll look in some detail at both viewpoint and developing characters later on, but for now there are some basic guidelines to explore.

Who is the main protagonist in this story? In other words, with which character do you as novelist have the most sympathy? With whom can you most identify or in whom are you most interested? As a first-time novelist, it's a good idea not to clutter your work with too many actors, and it's crucial that you pick the right main character for your purposes, or you may find that your book stutters to an untimely halt. This is not only important for you as a writer, but also for your reader. Even an anti-hero must engage our interest and to some extent our sympathy – we must want to know how he or she makes out.

Which brings us on to a brief look at viewpoint. In chapter seven we'll discuss the pros and cons of prospective viewpoints. For now, we'll explore the main possibilities.

The first and probably the most common as well as the easiest is that you follow the story through one person's eyes, but as if you're reporting. This will be a limited third-person narrative, and following the conventions we have talked about, you as narrator will have the ability to see inside this character's head and be privy to his or her feelings. The story you are telling will be unfolding from this character's perspective only, so that although you will be reporting on the actions of other characters, you will not be able to divine their feelings or unspoken thoughts, except inasmuch as they are reflected through the main character's perspective and experiences. In other words, you will only have access to the interior life of your main character.

The second is that you follow the main character's life in a first-person narrative, as if you are the 'I' of the story. You will have even less access to others' thoughts and actions, as you are limited to narrating only those scenes in which your protagonist is directly involved.

You may choose to follow two or more characters' stories with equal attention throughout the book; this is less easy to do convincingly, but it can work well as long as you show your readers your intention fairly early on, and keep some kind of consistency in the structure of the telling of the story; for instance, alternating chapters. This has its own challenges and requires a certain amount of (extra) skill and juggling.

The fourth main possibility is an extension of the third, where you as narrator take a 'god's-eye' view and dip in and out of as many characters' lives in as much detail as you wish – the so-called omniscient viewpoint.

The choice is of course your own, and some stories lend themselves to one way, others to another. Just be clear about which fits your ideas most nearly.

Past or present?

A further decision you will have to take on commencing your novel is whether you will be writing in the past or present tense. As a beginning writer you may find yourself switching between tenses unconsciously – keep an eye open for this. You can, of course, choose to set the main part of your story in the present tense, using the past tense in the case of flashbacks. As long as you are clear and your reader is clear about when the events depicted are happening, this works fine, but you're laying yourself open to the possibility of confusion, and good advice to a first-time novelist is to stick with one tense.

Which one? Once again, each has its strengths and weaknesses, as well as its advocates and opponents. The past tense is the most common and perhaps the smoothest; if the writing is strong enough we are held by the story and can immerse ourselves in it as if it were unfolding before our eyes. Its weakness is that it can lend a certain detachment to the reader, whereas a present-tense narrative is more immediate, arguably more grabbing. We can immerse ourselves in it. Many writers write successfully in the present tense; however, it's my impression that many readers dislike this device intensely. When we read, we understand that it's a 'given' that the story we are being asked to believe in has already happened; I'm not sure how much using the present tense help-fully adds to this. The governing criterion is surely whether the tense intrudes or obtrudes in any way. If it does, change it; or at least try another route.

Approaches to writing

Somerset Maugham said: 'There are three rules for writing a novel. Unfortunately, no-one knows what they are'. When it comes to writing, you're on your own, and it's a question of muddling through in whatever way suits you best. Ultimately, the process is alchemical rather than formulaic – provided you have roughly the right ingredients in roughly the right order and proportions and you are prepared to put in a lot of blood, sweat and tears and sprinkle on a good handful of inspiration and imag-ination, you're well on the way. Somewhere along the line you find you have shaken the bottle without really noticing and the thing starts to take shape.

It seems that writers divide roughly into four camps. There are those who plot, plan, structure and write hundreds of pages of notes before they even start to shape a novel from them. Their approach is often clear and objective and the form is easy, as virtu-ally all the work is done first.

There are those who just sit and write. They start with an inspired moment and just write from there, often without any idea of direction, shape, plot, outcome or even characters, trusting that these will appear as they write. If you are one of the latter type, you will know that almost miraculously the thing does take shape for you, without much apparent construction from you. This type worries about shape, structure and 'does it work?' only once the writing's been done. Unless, however, they're prepared to revise and redraft, they're often an editor's nightmare.

A third type writes key scenes, whether or not they are obviously connected. The hard slog, for them, involves linking the scenes in such a way as to make a story.

There's a fourth way, which is also my own. I have an idea of the main character or two, an intuition of the kinds of issues I want to explore, a rough outline in my head, or, better, on paper, and a sense of the ending. From there, I find a strong opening and beginning page, and let it write itself. It helps to be clear about plot and focus first, and early on — say around chapter three — I will make character-portraits of the two or three main people in my story. At around this time, too, I'll sketch out a synopsis from the chapter outlines detailed in chapter two.

You will know which approach will suit you best, and also which one it might be helpful to adopt.

Setting

The setting for your book, the backdrop against which the characters interact and the plot unfolds, is also an important consideration. Attention to setting will throw your story into relief, give it a three-dimensional shape, especially if you are able to conjure up sensory impressions for a reader. A book which does not build a setting has an unreal, shadowy quality to it which strains our credibility. Events never happen in a vacuum, but it's surprising how many new writers forget this.

E. Annie Proulx in her Pulitzer prizewinner *The Shipping News*, set in Newfoundland, sprinkles her narrative with frequent detailed but minimal descriptions of place, language used to capture scenes, smells, textures, mood:

> The short parade to Flour Sack Cove, take-out coffee slopping down dashboards, steering wheels gritty with doughnut sugar . . . The North tilted towards the sun. As the light unfolded, a milky patina of phytoplankton bloomed over the offshore banks along the collision line of the salt Gulf Stream and the brack Labrador Current . . . Rain-coloured distance . . . A deep smell to the air, some elusive taste that made him put in conscious breaths. Sky the straw-coloured ichor that seeps from a wound. Rust blossoms along the station wagon's door panels.

Throughout the book the harshness of the Newfoundland landscape and climate is contrasted with the fragility of human lives and loves:

> A few torn pieces of early morning cloud the shape and colour of salmon fillets. The tender greenish sky hardening as they drove between high snowbanks. A rim of light flooded up, drenched the car. Quoyle's yellow hands with bronze hairs, holding the wheel, Wavey's maroon serge suit like cloth of gold. Then it was ordinary daylight, the black and white landscape of ice, snow, rock and sky.

Whenever possible, choose settings that you know well and can picture. Readers are forgiving with certain parameters, as long as an author does not stretch beyond bounds their ability to believe in the book. However, setting a story in a location that the reader happens to know well when it is obvious that the writer does not, is virtually guaranteed to alienate or lose that reader. Make it your business to find out as much as you can about the place or places in which most of your action happens. There really is no substitute for a visit, preferably notebook and camera in hand. Drawing on childhood memories is not enough; if your book is set in the 1990s the playing-fields you remember may well have become a multi-storey car park, and the convent school metamorphosed into a block of flats.

It helps to have pictures of the setting, and maybe images related to it or photos of people who have some of the same physical characteristics as your characters in front of you as you write.

Bring yourself back frequently to imagined – or recorded – sense-impressions of the place. Try and construct pictures and images for your readers, bring the place alive (see the writing practice exercises at the end of this chapter). It's worth checking out how other writers tackle this. It doesn't take much to set a scene.

He'd left the open land behind him now. The city closed in. Waste lots. The desolate backs of tenements, row upon row, raw and unfinished, smoke-soiled, pipework bent and poking like fractured limbs. Rusty security fences impounding flattened scrap cars, naked in their uselessness. Gunmetal gas silos like strange preying giant insects from a nightmare future.

Noise pounded him on all sides; the rain drumming on the roof, battering the windscreen; the roar of the traffic and the nearby airport, and a deep electric thrumming which he imagined for a moment to be coming from the earth itself. He supposed it was the noise of the city, and the perpetual clashing of her inhabitants, life grinding on life. His heart was thumping with anticipation, with terror.

Take a look at these extracts from *As I Walked Out One Midsummer Morning* by that master of descriptive writing, Laurie Lee:

Then one day I noticed a long low cloud lifting slowly above the southern horizon, a purple haze above the quivering plain – the first sign of the approaching Sierras. After the monotonous wheatfields it was like a landfall, the distant coastline of another country . . . cool winds were blowing down from its peaks, and the plain was lifting into little hills, and by the next afternoon I'd left the

wheat behind me and entered a world of Nordic pinewoods. Here
I slipped off the heat like a sweat-soaked shirt and slept an hour
among the resinous trees – a fresh green smell as sweet as menthol
compared with the animal reek of the plain. I noticed that each
tree, slashed with a pattern of fishbone cuts, was bleeding gum into
little cups. The wounded trunks seemed to be running with drops
of amber, stinging the air with the piercing scent, while some of the
older trees, bled dry and abandoned, curled in spirals like burning
paper. But it was a good place to sleep; the wood was empty of flies,
who had learnt to avoid its sticky snares, and the afternoon sun
sucked up the flavour of each tree till the whole wood swam in
incense like a church.

Lee brings the same picture-conjuring talent to his descriptions
of humans, too, even secondhand, as it were:

> The deaf-mute boy Alonso, who I . . . met in the market and whose
> restless face and body built up images like a silent movie. He
> described his family in mime, patting their several heads, and
> suddenly one could see them in a row beside him – his handsome
> father, his coughing consumptive mother, fighting brothers and sly
> young sister. There was also a sickly baby, its head lolling back, and
> two dead ones, packed into little boxes – the boy set their limbs
> stiffly, sprinkled them with prayers, closed their eyes, and laid them
> away with a shrug.
>
> In the market, too, I met Queipo, a beggar, whose hand had been
> bitten off by a mad dog in Madrid. Sometimes he'd lift up the red
> and wrinkled stump, bare his teeth, and bark at it savagely.

Lee is here writing thirty years after the event, yet his writing
has the freshness, originality and vividness of imagery and language
which allows us to picture the scene as if he'd taken us by the hand
and led us to it in the here and now. He's not writing fiction –
except inasmuch as memory adds its own stories – but a fiction
writer needs to be equally able to paint these word-pictures.

How does Lee do it? One key is in his powerful use of observation; a reader feels as if Lee is at that moment standing in the wood, or communicating with Alonso. Surely Lee must take himself back to the time and place with all his senses as he writes. Then there is the use of imagery, metaphor and simile: 'I slipped off the heat like a sweat-soaked shirt'; the green smell of the pinewoods and the 'animal reek' of the plain; the 'fishbone cuts', and the sap like 'drops of amber'. He chooses his verbs with care; 'the afternoon sun *sucked* up the flavour', the trunks '*stinging* the air', Alonso '*sprinkling*' the dead babies with prayer. Despite his rich use of language, there is also an economy in it; in two sentences we have a clear and perfect picture of the most striking characteristics of Queipo the beggar.

Developing your eye and finding your voice

As a writer, all experience is grist to the mill. It's worth taking the time to capture scenes, thoughts, feelings, situations, conversations as soon as possible in words. You never know when you might be able to use them, and even if you don't, the practice is good for you. Train your eyes and ears to record. Explore how other writers do it, and experience what your own talents are. Perhaps you have an ear for humour or irony, perhaps you have a photographic memory, or a particular sensitivity to atmospheres – exploit these skills. Consciously try writing in a number of different styles and voices, switch perspectives from time to time and try looking out through another person's eyes at their world.

Often, we begin to write by imitating writers we admire. This is fine; it's only through writing that we begin to hear our own voice, find our own literary way. As you gain confidence in what you have to say, so you will also begin to trust the way in which you choose to say it.

I've talked a lot about decisions to be made before you start your novel. It's time, perhaps, to reiterate the need to differentiate between thinking about your writing and *doing* it. Of course a large part of the writing process involves the incubation of ideas, plotting, planning, thinking and rethinking. An even larger part means cajoling, threatening or rewarding yourself into getting the words down on paper, whether or not you know where you're going and regardless of whether you feel they're the right words. Just do it. It's no good waiting for the muse to appear like a genie out of a bottle; whilst she (or he) might grace you with an ephemeral presence, now and then, you can spend a lot of time attending on her, seducing her, pleading with her or even grabbing her by the throat and shutting her in with you. And there will be many, many times when she just doesn't respond, and you have to shut the door anyhow and get on with it.

Writing practice

Settings

Think of a place that you know and love well. Close your eyes and picture yourself in that place, absorbing all its details. Imagine that you want to describe it to someone dear to you, who is house-bound and blind. Write a description for them, based on what you see, hear, smell and can touch from your vantage point within that place.

Now do the same thing with a location you are using in your novel, whether it's real or imagined.

Plot versus character

Note down as many books as you can think of that you have read. Decide which of these is plot-driven, and which character-driven; how many are a balance of both?

Blurbs

Describe the essence of each of these books in between 150 and 200 words, as if you were writing the 'blurb' for the back jacket.

4 Inspiration, Observation, Imagination

Hunting and gathering

Ideas are everywhere, all the time. Everything, virtually, that we use, do or say has its inception in an idea. Some are great, some are not so wonderful. The point is, we live in a universe positively pulsating with ideas and possibilities.

The Oxford English Dictionary defines 'idea' thus.

- a conception or plan formed by mental effort
- a mental impression or notion; a concept
- a vague belief or fancy
- an intention, purpose or essential feature
- an archetype or pattern
- (philosophy) an externally existing pattern of which individual things in any class are imperfect copies
- a concept of pure reason which transcends experience

This is all right as far as it goes, which is not far enough. Let's stretch this a little further: I'm going to define 'idea' in terms of creative writing as including 'the originating spark' and 'a flash of inspiration'. In these definitions, idea has more in common with imagination than it does with reason, which is, I believe, how it should be.

Ideas, as I've already suggested, are a little like wild animals. Stalking them requires practice and patience, and a willingness to acquaint yourself over a period of time with their habits and behaviour, their signs and preferred times of day. Once you start to track animals, the forest comes alive for you in a way you would never have dreamed possible in the days when you weren't looking for them. It's a bit like driving a slightly obscure foreign car: until you possess one, you never see them; then suddenly the roads are congested with them. 'So much of seeing,' someone remarked, 'is looking for the expected, and tuning out the rest.' In order to open channels to the imagination, the natural realm of ideas, you need to unlearn old patterns and teach yourself different methods of perception. You need to train your eyes and your ears to be on the alert, and your normal mode of being may need to be left on one side.

Ideas are also seeds. Behind every creative work is the tiniest germ of an idea; the time and effort and patience and willingness to make compost and dig it in is what will allow this seed to develop its potential, once you've recognized it for what it is.

The problem for a writer is twofold: first, learning to perceive or receive ideas; secondly, finding a container or vehicle, a shape, for them once you've caught them.

I talked in chapter one about cultivating the ground of ideas through dreams, paying attention to feelings and moods, participating in activities which involve the senses and which feed the imagination; and in chapter two we looked at stream-of-consciousness writing. All these things help to open doors so that ideas may stream through to you. A bit like attending a jumble sale or going through a ragbag, there will be many you will discard; amongst them, though, you're more likely than not to find a piece of rare silk, some fancy buttons, maybe even a decent overcoat.

You should by now have a journal for writing practice. If you haven't already, you need now to buy a smallish, fattish notebook which you carry with you at all times. This is purely for jottings:

notes and ideas, scraps. In it will go words, phrases, lines, thoughts, imaginings, overheard or even misheard snippets, quotes, inspirations, observations, details, song lines, crazinesses. Think of this as your ragbag, or your 'rainy day notebook'.

Ideas, once recorded on paper, have a delightful knack of growing all by themselves. It's as if the act of putting them down on paper gives them permission to take shape. They take on a reality of their own. Many a novel has started in this way. Try and resist the temptation to keep reading back over your notes. Some germination has to start in the dark, and it never will if you keep digging the seeds up to check for roots. Allow some time to elapse, or use the notebook to dip into at random on the days when all inspiration for writing practice has fled you.

Sources for stories

A good guideline for the fiction writer is 'tell it like it isn't'. The art of telling it like it is belongs to non-fiction. Telling the truth is an exact science, like photojournalism; fiction is more like painting, ranging from the impressionistic to the purely abstract. The fiction writer transforms fact into something other: how it could be, how it might have been. If you do not innately have the knack of embroidery and exaggeration, you might want to try and acquire it. Embroidery, whatever you might feel about it morally in the 'real world', is what turns an anecdote into a story. Most novels are a blend of fact and fiction, one way or another.

Where do we go for our stories? Well, life: our own, our friends' and family's (but be careful), our neighbours', our community's, the wider world . . . stories are everywhere. Take a headline at random. Don't read the text; make up your own. (Thriller writer Richard Doyle wrote a whole book from one line in the *Daily Telegraph*.) Flip through a problem page in a magazine, or the personal columns of a paper. Let your imagination create a scenario from a vignette. Go to Shakespeare, the

Bible, mythology, fairy tales (Angela Carter and Margaret Atwood do this well), Ovid, Malory, Homer, anthropology, travel stories. Take a moment or an event in history. Rewrite the Gallic Wars or the story of Antony and Cleopatra as if you were a reporter from the *Sun* (though I'm not necessarily suggesting this would make good literature, only offering different ways of looking at events).

Remake it all. Define the theme, lift it, put it into a new story, a new venue, a new cast, a different time. Take an intriguing snippet of conversation, invent a context and a set of players. 'Borrow' from the subtexts in films or plays or musicals or even books. Tell the stories that *weren't* told (e.g. Stoppard's *Rosencrantz and Guildenstern Are Dead*). What about the rest of the lives of the two ugly sisters? How could you make the Pied Piper of Hamelin into a contemporary story?

In Kieslowski's three films based on the colours of the French flag, there's a tiny recurring motif which appears to have no relevance to the main text: a minute unidentified elderly woman attempting to reach on tiptoe to deposit her bottle in the bottle bank and failing, until finally, she manages it. (In the cinema where I saw the films, you could tell who had seen the previous ones from the small cheer that went up in the audience.) One day, I'll write her story.

Novelists are pretty shameless, really. Everything's a potential source: it's as if we drag a trawl through our lives with us. And why not? They say there's nothing new under the sun; it's a question of recreating it in the most original way possible. You can write about anything, as long as it intrigues you, arouses your curiosity or your wonder.

Other sources include your dreams and memories, your fantasies and your emotions. Write about a loss, an early memory, an embarrassment, a conflict. Write out a dream. Exaggerate. Try writing it in the immediacy of a dialogue – invent characters, invent a context, invent their history. Put it all in your ragbag rainy day notebook, let it incubate.

Powers of observation

So your ragbag contains a selection of scraps of the richest colours and textures. You need to put into this bag your observations as well as your recordings and imaginings. This means that when you pull out a scrap of fabric which may well be a thread from the gown of the visiting Queen of Sheba at the court of Solomon, you have the powers to describe the gown, the Queen and the court in a way that enables your audience to participate in your imaginings. In other words, you need to add substance to your imaginings; the substance of the material world. Exactly *what* shade of blue? What does it resemble? What does its texture remind you of? How does the gown hang?

If creative writing is a blend of imagination, observation, experience and 'factor X', you can at least develop your imagination and observational skills to the point at which the visitation of the unquantifiable 'factor X' is a frequent possibility (experience, of course, is a given).

Learn how to really look. You can help this process along by practising unaccustomed ways of looking. A useful exercise for painters is to spend time looking at the shapes made by the gaps *between* objects. Somehow it enables you to see the object itself more clearly, as if it brings it into focus. It's useful, too, for a writer for at least two reasons: one, it helps train your eye to look in a different way, looking for the unexpected, the unnoticed; two, it helps to set an object in context, it gives it a place in an overall scheme. It's easy, as a writer, to focus on foreground, on object or event, and forget that the imagined and described scene does not happen in a vacuum.

When you write from observation, try and describe exactly the scene or object or person or event in front of you, just as it is. Imagine you're perceiving it for the very first time and have no preconceptions or expectations to bring to it. Just note its characteristics. This is the equivalent of painting a detailed representational still life; it may have its limitations, but it's invaluable in terms of developing your eye and your hand to work in tandem.

You may want to bring a discipline to this kind of observation. Perhaps one day's observation exercises could focus on skin: the skin of a person, of an animal, of a fruit, of a tree, of a building. Another day you may want to note exactly how many different shades of green there are in the garden or the park, or write about a square foot of rock on the cliff path, or what happens to the muscles in your toes, your feet, your ankles, your calves, hips, knees each time you take a step. Or you could try tuning out the other senses and focusing just on sound. Write about the clatter of a metal dustbin lid, about traffic and aeroplanes and birds, about the thin wail of the next-door baby, about a thrush cracking a snail on a stone, about the sounds of cooking, typing, bathwater running, about the audience at a football match or swimmers in a pool. Listen to individual voices, listen to the whole massed choir of the world going on all around you. This is not, remember, about flights of fancy, the soaring heights of the imagination; purely a discipline in really seeing, hearing, recording things exactly as they are. Be precise.

Bringing the threads together

Imaginings, we could say, belong to our interior world. Observation is objective perception of the outer world: 'the act of noticing', 'the accurate watching and noting of phenomena as they occur'. The written word, in the case of the former, translates flights of fancy, feelings, fantasies, possibilities into a series of concrete marks on paper; in the case of the latter, it changes the solidly concrete form of external 'evidence' into a less objectively verifiable paper record. Creative writing, perhaps, consists of finding ways of linking the two.

The sometimes incoherent nature of our untrammelled imaginative ramblings, consisting, as it so often does in its rather dream-like way, of absurdities, sideways leaps and apparently unconnected imagery, can benefit from the structuring of factual reportage. Equally the latter, if it is not to end up as a dry rational piece of documentation which has little place in *creative* expression, needs the vitality and fire of the imagination.

A good practice is to switch between the two modes of perception – the one connected with intuition, the other connected with sensation – as an exercise (see 'Writing practice' below). You can write a piece firmly in one mode, then another piece from the other perspective. For our purposes here, it's worth differentiating and sticking strictly to each one in its own time. Say, for example, you're sitting on a park bench. In your first piece of writing, timed at five minutes, you record, as an impartial observer, all that you can perceive happening in the outside world around you. This includes 'static' happenings – noting the texture of the bench on which you're sitting, its feel against your clothes or your body, the colour or patterns of the leaves against the sky, the warmth of the sun on your hair as well as the blue-black gloss of the beetle crawling over your foot and the rhythmic thud of a jogger's trainers hitting tarmac.

In your second piece of writing, you are recording on paper the fleeting impressions, feelings and images thrown up from your inner world. You are still timing yourself, you are still sitting on your park bench, but the focus of your writing is totally inward. In our culture introspection is not generally given a high value or much time, so initially the act of looking inward may prove tricky. This can be cultivated, and activities such as yoga, tai chi and meditation all facilitate this, as does time alone.

These disciplines will have a different flavour, depending on whether you are in a building or outside. Try both.

The third way most nearly approaches the final objective of rounded fiction in which we are able to portray realistically the 'interior life' of our characters, and create a substantial world in which they move, eat, drink, love, hate and go about the business of living.

This can also form a useful exercise, where we allow our attention to be in two places at once – the outer world of stimuli and the inner one of response. Here we are recording in a more or less cohesive whole the events as registered camera-like by our powers of observation, and our feelings, images and imaginings in relation to them.

The simple observation of a dog, for instance, may conjure up different feeling responses in the observer. Noting these down in addition to the recording of the factual details – a large, hairy black-and-brown dog is barking and racing after a stick – will add a depth and an individuality to a written record. Perhaps the observer has recently lost a dog, and views the scene with a sad nostalgia; perhaps she has a deep distrust and fear of dogs, having been mauled by one as a toddler; perhaps he is a photographer who is captivated by the movement and vitality of the moment and views the scene aesthetically; perhaps she is a dog-hater whose response to 'dog' merely conjures up disgust and annoyance at the possibility of treading in dog-muck. Each person, then, will paint a different word-picture of this moment.

One of the bridges we make between the two worlds – observation and imagination, outer and inner – is likening something to something else. The object or event unfolding in front of us tugs, perhaps, the memory of a similar event or a similar feeling response in the 'I' who is observing and recording, and another time or place with its own set of events and responses suddenly emerges into the picture. This lateral approach adds another dimension.

In terms of the use of language, simile and metaphor can perform the function of linking the two worlds of observation and imagination. The observational method notes, say, that a dandelion is a bright yellow disc with a number of petals striking out all around it. The imagination may describe it as butter-yellow – butter being a metaphor used as an adjective – and liken it to the sun or a golden brooch or halo. Butter, sun, brooch, halo then all have their own connotations which they bring to the equation. Memory may offer other dimensions; perhaps as a child you kept a tortoise, and watched its slow, deliberate tongueing of dandelion flowers into its mouth. Maybe your father used to collect dandelions to make wine. Perhaps your association is in the present, with a feeling response – maybe they herald spring after a particularly difficult winter. Allow all these things to make themselves felt; allow your written world to be three-dimensional. If you can bring all these different aspects into your fiction-writing, you have a greater chance of creating for the reader a fuller picture of the moment than he or she would have if it had been merely a factual record, or only the promptings of someone's imagining with no anchor in the external world.

As always, of course, you can overdo it; try to strive for balance between simplicity and imagery.

Here are two extracts from a workshop, the first written inside a building, the second outside but with the attention confined to a very small area. Both allow an interplay between observation and imagination, but are rooted in the physical world.

I've come back inside after 'taking my mind for a walk'. So here; flowers a foot from my nose and a trio of glorious dancing swans, wooden and elegant, in front of the window.

This table has eyes; the flowers have eyes. Even the vase; golden eyes like a lion's. I feel warmed, feeling the world is looking at me as I am looking at it.

So many shapes. The rhomboids and rectangles of this simple vase, a surprising triangulated top, dashed yellow shapes. The squared lines of chairs and tables. The dipped ceiling with gold and green scrolled border, interlocking curves. The following smoothness of swan-shapes, the waves of wood-grain.

A waft of wood-smoke and sweet honeyed narcissus.

To be bursting out into this beautiful spring abundance.

And then I am lost in the eye of the tulip. A seven-petalled extravagance of blazing scarlet, daring and passionate, veined with darker crimson, pooled where petals overlap like layers of tissue-paper. A tide-line of palest pink and then an abrupt zigzagged interruption of lemon-yellow and a startling streaked blue-green starry centre, like a frozen moment from a kaleidoscope. The petals are waxen, silky like thigh-skin; polished into a sheen where the light lies across them. Springing from the centre a black spiky crown, seven-legged like a spider just escaped with its life at the price of a leg. Out of this an arising, a triangular pistil, fleshy-pink and tipped. Crown and sceptre. A scattering of pollen.

I tear my eyes away; smell coffee, stand and stretch.

Outside again, and the eyes here, too – the watcher being watched. Choosing a couple of feet of wall an interesting confinement for me; a discipline in seeing. Not so much for my senses to roll in, drown in. Yet a million eyes in this surface; the eyes of holes, small holes where insects live, bigger ones at foot and roof. The eyes of lichen; ancient, slow, creeping feet claiming surfaces for their own, millimetre by millimetre. These eyes are rough but soft; silvery, olive, orange like dried egg-yolk, whitened like bleached bones.

Then the eyes of light and shade, protrusions pronounced, hollows and caverns thrown into darkness, lips into relief. Sandy to touch, barnacled; lines and small clefts and escarpments deflecting the fingers, running shivers up the skin. Close to the lichen is webbed and fronded like seaweed, puckered and creased, spread-eagled. I remember someone telling me that lichen is a cross between algae and fungus. Umbers, ochres, pinky-reds, slate-greys; shine of mica winking in the sun.

A million eyes, all watching me as I am watching them.

Writing with all the senses

An important component of most novels is what we might call the life of the senses. A fiction writer's success is intimately bound up with the skill he or she has for creating pictures in the mind of the reader. The physical world and the ability of the author to conjure up views, smells, sounds, textures and even tastes for a reader cannot be over-emphasized. This talent can and must be cultivated;

this is what will make a book three-dimensional, and give substance to its characters.

Good creative writing is firmly rooted in the world of the senses, and in the particular, says Julian Birkett in *Word Power*, rather than in generalized notions; in the concrete, not the abstract. A piece of writing which refers back to sense-impressions almost always has more impact than a piece of writing that is abstract. More of us, our being, both as reader and writer, is engaged in the former. 'What we respond to, with our senses as well as our minds, is a dramatic reconstruction of reality rather than an essay about it . . . the writing process is as much concerned with transformation of experience as with mere description.' The value, says Birkett, of a piece of writing is determined by whether it enables us to look at things with a fresh eye.

John Moat, the co-founder of the Arvon Foundation, said once that when he begins a piece of creative writing he makes a note of the five senses – seeing, hearing, tasting, touching, smelling – at the top right of the page he's working on. He'll refer back to this frequently, to anchor his writing. This is a good habit to adopt, certainly until it becomes second nature to use the senses as a component of language.

One way of practising this – second only to doing it with 'the real thing' – is to use a photograph or a postcard as a starting point for a narrative sketch, or a poem if that's your inclination. Take yourself into the scene depicted in your imagination, and recreate that scene in glorious 3D. What kinds of sounds would you hear? What are the main colours and shapes? Textures? What physical sensations might you feel? Any particular odours or scents? (Taste is not always as appropriate, but there are some scents – like salt wind – that you taste; or maybe the picture incorporates food or drink.) Write a few sentences for each sense, until you have built the world of the picture around you. You may want to stop there, or you may want to develop this into a piece of prose by asking yourself questions like: What's happening now? Why? What if? Who?

Grist to the mill

For a writer, everything's grist to the mill. Into the mill go observations and imaginings, and also of course our experiences. With the possible exception of potboilers written with a specific purpose – normally to make money – and therefore to a specific format, a novel will tend to reflect, even if only indirectly, a writer's own experiences and interests, and the picture of the world thus formed. Writing a novel is a way of making and remaking the world, for the author as much as the reader.

The seed-idea for many writers comes as a fragment of memory; an observed or experienced incident fleshed out in the imagination with the writer's key question: what if? What if an argument that you had with your brother *hadn't* been resolved in half an hour or two days, but had continued fermenting over months or years? What if you, or your brother, had a different temperament which spilt over into easy violence? What if the argument hadn't been about who won the squash game but about the arguably more serious implications of rivalry over a woman? What if the hidden agenda was that you were in love with your brother's wife?

Or let's say you have a strange experience in a foreign town, maybe an incident of *déjà vu*. Maybe you discover – or just imagine – later that there was a mystery of some kind surrounding the spot of your experience, maybe an unsolved murder. What if you accidentally and innocently stumble upon hidden evidence? Or what if you discover in yourself psychic powers which enable you to step back in time, or read others' minds? What if you become privy through these powers to suppressed information?

In this way, the incident, fairly minor in itself, can grow into a whole story. A prizewinning short story of my own, *Anniversary*, had at its core a theme from legend: the idea of a seal-woman. I set the story on an unspecified Scottish island and in the present day, and wrote it in such a way that it could be read simultaneously as an exploration of a marriage in the somewhat harsh climate of a northern island crofting lifestyle, and a story which hinted at supernatural explanations for the wife's appearance and disappearance. I like the idea of things not being as they seem. I drew on my own experiences and observations of a rural smallholding lifestyle, of the differing needs which partners may bring to a marriage and of an impression connected with scenery and atmosphere of a number of islands, some Scottish. I brought to this my love of rural landscapes and careful observation, and I clearly used my imagination to construct the story. The selkie or seal-woman idea presented itself about a page into the writing, at which point I rewrote the opening paragraph.

The originating spark, though, the seed-idea, came simply from two sentences plucked, as they say, out of thin air, which I set a writing group as an opening: 'It was high tide. At the water's edge, slightly salt-stained and still laced up, stood a pair of shoes.'

Pain and passion

Writing is an emotional, exposing business. If it has any substance to it, if it is to make an impact on a reader, you are likely to invest quite a lot of yourself in the writing. This risk-taking is a crucial part of the business. Whether or not you write directly about feelings, in a piece of creative writing you will need to be able to draw on your feeling experiences in order to create your characters and the events in their world.

Into the ragbag must go, with your imaginings and ideas, observations and sources, your feelings. It's quite cathartic on a personal level, too, to be able to write out your anger and your pain, your joy and your love, your doubts and fears. Easier said than done, I know, but it will help your writing along tremendously – not to mention your psychological health – if you allow yourself to really *feel* your feelings. Our culture doesn't easily encourage this. So when you get the chance, preferably as soon as you feel able after an 'emotional event', note down the incident and your feelings about it, as well as the physical sensations involved. Nobody else will see your notebook; and you never know when you might be able to draw on this and translate the incident into the life of one of your characters.

I am clearly not suggesting that a novel is an undigested mush of feelings. A perennial problem for the writer, too, is how to write about love and grief without falling into sentimentality. Often understatement works best – the gently direct matter-of-fact tone such as Michael Ondaatje uses in *The English Patient* when he's describing the burnt body of the main character and the responses of his self-appointed nurse can convey worlds of pain and compassion (see chapter eight).

Dan Franck, in *Separation*, employs this somehow slightly distant reporting tone throughout the whole book, which is what it says it is: a record of the last stages of a marriage. And yet we are drawn in to the agony of the couple, especially the man, from whose perspective the book is written. We *know* how he feels; by a clever combination of choice of incident – most of us can relate to the sense that someone is withdrawing from us, even if only through a distant adolescent memory – and the perceptiveness that comes either from having experienced it, or something like it, or from a profound understanding of human psychology, he enables us to step right into this man's head. And yet the writing is simple and unadorned; in fact he breaks many of the 'rules' that I've suggested. It's all foreground; he pays little attention to setting or context or sensory detail. Everything is subservient to the main thrust of the story, to which he brings an extraordinary feeling of intensity. It's a very un-English book (the author is in fact French).

Hanging out

So, in summary, much of what I have said about the creative writing process is about re-educating ourselves to really look, really listen, really hear, really feel. A writer's antennae need to be on constant alert, feeling out all possibilities, registering and logging them.

Keep your writer's ears and eyes with you at all times, along with the ubiquitous notebook. Cafés, bars, trains, buses, parks, parties all offer opportunities, potential stories. Get into the habit of noting down anything at all which catches your attention, however irrelevant it seems at the time. Like adding hot water to packet soup – but more exciting – a 'what if' sprinkled at a later stage onto a mere crumb of sentence may suddenly produce a snack, if not a meal.

This, of course, is a wonderful justification to do what the non-writing world thinks writers do all the time – spend a great deal of time over endless cups of coffee or glasses of beer listening in on other people's conversation, in the hopes of gleaning the perfect story.

Writing practice

Taking your mind for a walk

Choose a favourite walk. Stop at three key points for ten minutes each. At the first, concentrate on the wide picture only, and make an accurate record of all that you see and hear from this spot, including your general impressions of the landscape.

At the second point, concentrate on a very small area in close-up. Study this in detail, and note as much of it down as you can in ten minutes. Surprisingly, though the area is small, you will find that the more you look, the more you will see, and ten minutes may not feel enough.

At the third key point, allow yourself to become part of the picture rather than an observer, and record your feelings, impressions and responses to the landscape around you, allowing your imagination to suggest twists and turns and interpretations and perspectives.

You might like to take this walk in other weather, different times of day (or night) and other seasons, stopping at the same key points.

Objects – three exercises in perspective

Collect together two or three natural objects, such as shells, fruit, feathers, pebbles, fossils, pine cones, dried seed cases and the like. (You can, if you choose, include man-made objects like buttons or shoe-brushes or kitchen utensils.)

For each one, write three short pieces. All three require that you approach this object as if seeing it for the first time.

The first is an exact, almost scientific, objective description of the object, as if logging it for research cataloguing. Be as accurate as possible – if it's brown, exactly what shade of brown? Use as many senses as appropriate to give a full picture.

The second is the opposite. Imagine you are a visitor from another time or another planet who has never seen an object like this before. Allow your imagination free rein, let in curiosity and wonder. What might this object be? What can it do? How does it move? What could its function or purpose be?

The third is to assume the voice of this object (write in the first person) and address the world from its perspective. Rather like a riddle, the idea is to paint as full a picture as possible whilst still being somewhat lateral, obscure. If you prefer, choose a different object, such as a lobster pot, mug, ladder, coathook. Allow your imagination to go to town – be as pretentious as you like. Here is an example.

> I spend most of my life upside down. The one good thing is that the colour of my hair changes a lot – not that I've much say in it. If they forget to clean me I have the mother-and-father of a hangover the next day – so stiff there's no moving me.
>
> The not-so-good bits are all that wiggling to fill my hair up – breathing's not so easy – and then they beat hell out of me against

the wall for half a minute before dunking me back under. Don't ask my why – strange things, humans.

(This is a paintbrush, if you hadn't guessed.)

Four fifteen-minute exercises

- Write about a loss.
- Write about an early memory.
- Write out a dream.
- Write out the record of a conflict or disagreement you've recently had.

What if?

Take a strong emotion – fear, anger, jealousy, lust, betrayal, joy etc.

1 Write about it from personal experience. Try and relive it as you write; record remembered physical sensations as well as the intensity of the emotion.
2 Write about it as if it were an animal.
3 Use it as the core of a fictitious short story. Add a 'what if . . .'. Give the emotion to a different person in a different situation, but try and retain the intensity. Use the above notes if you like.

5 Right-brain Writing

Creativity and feeling

The momentous work done earlier this century by Dr Jung suggested that our 'normal' waking consciousness is only the tiny tip of an iceberg, or a small island in a vast ocean. The king of this island, the ruling force, is the ego; and surrounding this field of self-consciousness is the sea of the unconscious. Or, if you prefer, it is the enormous mass that forms the body of the iceberg.

For most of us, as I've mentioned, our main contact with the unconscious is through the realm of dreams. We meet it, too, through art and works of the imagination: paintings, music, theatre, story, dance.

Now and then it intrudes into our daily life – through daydreams for instance. Another example is when something stirs our feelings; we've all had the experience of finding ourselves delivering a sudden, passionate outburst on something that has without warning touched our feelings. We can all find ourselves, from time to time, caught up in strange moods, inexplicable depressions, feelings that seemed to descend on us from nowhere. Most of us, too, can recall a time when we've suddenly been affected by an atmosphere.

Once or twice, no doubt, you've been running through a scenario, a memory or a problem in your mind whilst driving; you arrive at your destination and realize that you have no idea how you got there. You've taken the necessary turns, stopped at the necessary lights and pedestrian crossings and found the correct roads; and yet when you get there you have no memory of the journey at all. No, I'm not talking about abduction by aliens – though there might be an explanation here somewhere for so-called abductions – but about 'automatic pilot'. Whilst your conscious mind was engaged in something absorbing, your unconscious mind stepped in and did the necessary work.

There are those times, too, when a scent, a word, a scene will provoke a long-lost memory or feeling, or an image.

The ego is somewhat threatened by the apparent chaos of this turbulent, untrammelled world. The ego likes to be in control, to have the reins tightly in hand, to steer and direct our lives towards survival. This part of ourselves doesn't really like to take too many risks; anything new and untried is perceived as possibly dangerous. It prefers things which can be easily categorized and which make sense and proceed in an orderly manner towards a predictable outcome. Its survival instinct is strong.

The function of normal consciousness – which is of course necessary – can also be labelled, for our purposes, 'left brain'. Left brain is logical, reasoning, linear and sequential, orderly. Left brain oversees our powers of discernment and discrimination. It deals in intellectual processes, progressions, critical functions and objectivity.

In our culture and our educational system, left brain is highly valued. Goal-orientated, it 'gets things done'. Its shortcoming – and its enemy – is the intuitive world of feelings, instincts and imagination.

Our creativity and our capacity to imagine, to feel, to love, are linked to another part of ourselves. The 'right brain' part of us, the world of the unconscious, actually provides the nourishment for all that we are, including the world of the ego, the conscious mind. They are not separate, although in the West we have forgotten to some extent how to move between them, how to build bridges.

One of the demands for a writer – and many writers manage this intuitively – is to move back and forth between these two worlds. We convert impressions into expressions. If we do it well, our work can offer a bridge for a reader to do the same. Deep down, we all have a yearning to lose ourselves – even momentarily – in this other world, this world of dreams and images, away from the 'red alert' state of the conscious mind. This is crucial, in fact, for health; a study a few years ago showed this. A number of student volunteers were monitored whilst sleeping. Although given enough sleep in terms of hours, they were woken up every time they entered a period of REM (rapid-eye-movement) sleep, the mode in which dreams occur. After a number of days of this, the subjects started hallucinating. The brain needs this vital recharging; if it doesn't get it in the normal way, it finds another route.

So where left brain is logical, right brain is irrational. Where left brain is reasonable and orderly (I have a theory that left-brain-ruled cultures developed queuing), right brain is emotional and chaotic. Where left brain is literal, right brain is lateral. Left brain needs to make sense and be grown-up; right brain needs wild flights of fancy and time to play. Right brain offers the images; left brain interprets and shapes them.

If left brain is critic, right brain is creator. The interaction between the two produces works of art. If the right prompts and inspires, the left channels and shapes. We need both; and we especially need to learn to access the right brain if we want our written work to be vital, exciting, surprising, original, and to have depth.

Chatterboxes and control freaks

The inspiring tutor Natalie Goldberg talks of 'monkeymind' and 'tidy mind'. These are good metaphors for two states of mind beyond which creative writers need to be able to travel.

Monkey mind is incessantly busy. It collects to itself and slavers over absolutely everything, soaking up information like a sponge, indiscriminately and voraciously. Much of what it devours – most, even – is trivial. Bombarded as we are with a constant stream of stimuli, our minds work overtime digesting the information and filtering out and processing what seems to be important. I'm reminded of the mussel, through whose shell about ten gallons of water pass a day in order for it to filter out the small quantity of minute particles on which it feeds. (An image offered by the right brain there.)

Monkey mind is the chatterbox. Monitor yourself for five minutes. There is constant 'white noise' which passes for thought – snippets of more important thoughts interspersed with a barrage of 'where did I put that?', 'is there time for this?', 'maybe a cup of tea', 'what shall I have for supper?', 'did she really mean that?', 'don't like his tie very much', 'must get in touch with . . .', 'damn, forgot to cancel the newspapers', 'that's a book I'd like to read', 'what was that noise?', 'looks like she's going to be late again'. You get the picture. We all do it. There is a connection here with what we discussed in chapter two, what has been called 'stream-of-consciousness' writing as exemplified by Virginia Woolf and James Joyce (though it is not exactly synonymous with what I mean by this). Here our view of the interior life of a character involves their interior monologue, too. Clearly, there is some selection going on in Woolf's and Joyce's writing in order to make the flow smooth and not too tedious.

Tidy mind is the control freak, the critic. This is the little voice – or sometimes a very loud one – that says: 'You can't write that. It doesn't make sense. Your mother-in-law might read it. You're writing rubbish. You'll never make a writer. What does that mean? Who do you think's going to want to read this? Go on, bin it.' Tidy mind – the critic – does have a part to play in writing, but in an editorial capacity *after* the creative work has been done. The critic/editor helps shape and structure the images and ideas in order to present them as clearly as possible with a view to conveying them to an audience.

Somehow you as writer need to find a way to bypass these two modes of thought, to find a path between them to what you actually want to say, to what is important.

The critic seems to respond well to being told to stay out of the way for a period of time. You can use psychological 'tricks' – Natalie Goldberg talks about visualizing sending the critic to the day-care centre while you get on with your creative writing! With groups I've found a useful image is to ask people to picture themselves leaving the critic outside the door of the writing room, which is then shut. The critic is only invited in when you want an editorial eye, and then dismissed again. Treat the internal critic as you would a well-meaning but overbearing and interfering busybody of a neighbour. 'I don't need your help right now, thank you.' You can always make a deal that you'll let the critic have a look-in later. Bribe him or her. This psycho-speak may all seem a bit over the top, but indulge it, play it up, make characters out of these internal functions. The right brain loves games like these.

The writer's use of meditation

I can't emphasize enough how helpful some kind of meditation process is in stilling the chatterbox. Though it's hard sometimes, especially at the beginning, learning to still and slow the mind pays dividends in many different areas.

One payoff is that, deprived of its habitual stimulus, monkey mind eventually goes to sleep for a while, though it has to be said not always without a grumble.

Meditation is not about suppressing anything. Meditation here is about finding ways of making a path through all the trivia to what lies underneath. It involves gaining a sense of proportion, and allowing other parts of the brain to come in. It enables the mind to change gear. It's not achieved by pushing out the unwanted thoughts; it's achieved by allowing them to pass by without grabbing at them, without attaching any importance to them in any way at all.

If this appeals to you, here are some suggestions.

Find yourself a quiet place and a time when a minimum of interruption will occur. You might want to unplug the phone and lock the front door.

Find a position that's comfortable. You have two options: to sit up or to lie down. They offer different things. If you lie down, the brain may get the message that you want to go to sleep. While this will be relaxing, it's not quite the same as meditating. On the other hand, when you're lying down the messages sent to the brain may allow you easier access to the unconscious, as is the case immediately before and after sleep. If you sit up, you are less likely to fall asleep and more likely to be in control. One way around this is to use the supine position for active imagination or visualizations (of which more later) and the sitting one for the purpose of stilling your mind.

If you sit, choose a comfortable chair which supports you upright. It's best if your surroundings, or at least your immediate view, aren't too interesting, unless you're going to close your eyes (which helps the process). Some people use something like a candle-flame as a focus – with their eyes open of course. Another way is just to bring your attention to your breath; just noticing the breath coming into the body and the breath leaving the body. Each time your mind wanders – and it does – just gently bring your attention back to the breath. Don't allow your critic in to berate you about this. If your mind wanders, you're not 'doing it wrong', you haven't failed – it's just the way the mind is. A meditation teacher I once had suggested picturing the mind as a wide blue sky, and the thoughts as clouds floating across it, which you notice but don't either hang on to or push away.

Each time it becomes a little easier; your attention span lengthens. As thoughts and feeling arise, notice them and let them pass by. You may find some useful images and ideas; you may not. The point is to still the surface chatter so that you can look beneath. The sense of relaxation and wellbeing is a bonus!

If you can, do this every day, starting with ten minutes and building up to as long as is comfortable. It's a good discipline to do immediately before writing, especially if you have got into the habit of stream-of-consciousness writing in the way that we explored in chapter two. You can use the meditation experience